Foundations

From ? ? Bennett
The Best
of Astrology
to you!
April 2018

Naomi Bennett

ISBN 978-1-892134-02-8

Publisher: BonAmi Publishing, Austin, Texas

Library of Congress Control Number 2014919087

Acknowledgements

"The real voyage of discovery consists not in seeking new landscapes but in having new eyes." - Marcel Proust

"Man is the measure of all things" - Heraclitus

"All is Angle" - Ancient Egyptian Saying

"If you want to find the secrets of the universe, think in terms of energy, frequency and vibration." - Nicolas Tesla

Special thanks go to my daughter, Adrianne Ondarza for her editing talents as a creative writer and my spouse, Bobby Bennett for his tolerance and support. Additional thanks goes to Ehsan Khazeni for his technical expertise and support.

Gratitude is given for all astrological researchers before me especially Carl Payne Tobey. I stand on the shoulders of giants to see further.
                            ~

Many of the images were acquired in the public domain using Wikipedia Commons which is a great gift to the world. Videos are from YouTube.

Horoscopes were generated using Solar Fire Gold by Esoteric Technologies and AstroDeluxe by John Halloran, precession images generated by StarWalk and Skyglobe. Bold text is the author's to highlight important passages.

Cover image was designed by the author. An Egyptian Pharaoh is standing with the Goddess Seshat, the goddess of measurements, writing and libraries. She was the precursor to Thoth. They are 'stretching the cords' to lay the foundation of a temple aligned with the Ursa Major, the Big Dipper which contained the Ecliptic North Pole at one point.

The title page shows the Goddess Nut drawn on the inside lid of a sarcophagus in the Hellenistic Greek period in Coptic Egypt. The dead could look up to the sky, which was the domain of Nut.

Table of Contents

Introduction

I and most other astrologers were highly influenced by our teachers and mentors. "We are a product of our times and of the many astrologers that have come before us". I feel my current knowledge of astrology is not only based on experience but that I stand on the shoulders of astrologers that have come before me. There is a deep and profound knowledge in the astrology of life and human behavior that was left for us to decipher and re-discover for our times. For instance, changing discoveries in the sciences have greatly improved our lives and health in medicine to the point that physical death as it was known in the astrological sense can no longer be predicted as it was centuries ago. A difficult Saturn transit could be a slow death or a long-term illness. Now with modern medicine, techniques and medicines can pull a patient from the brink of terminal death to prolonged life. The psychological nature of the aspect such as a long Saturn transit is still true: confinement, limitations and frustrations are likely to happen but the death part is not predictable.

In the USA there was a huge revival of astrology that started with the Theosophist Society beginning in 1875 until Helena Blavatsky's death in 1891, when the society broke apart into various factions (Krishnamurti dissolved the American branch in 1925).[1] It was in the early 1930's that a new generation of New York astrologers started taking astrology apart to find out what worked and what didn't. It started with Sydney K. Bennett (Wynn's Astrology) and then centered with Grant Lewi since he was editor of so many of the American astrology magazines. Lewi was a close friend with Carl Payne Tobey (my mentor) and a cluster of male astrologers that wrote for the magazines Lewi edited like Charles Jayne and Dane Rudhyar. A review of who and what entails modern astrology is discussed in James Holden's book, A *History of Horoscopic Astrology*.[2] Since the 1990s there has been a trend to re-translate old astrological texts and re-define traditional astrology. I'm hoping that we are at a point where a marriage of the traditional with the modern can create a working whole but I think it will take another twenty years for the next generation of astrologers to finish this integration.

The invention of home computing and the ability of modern astrologers to use astrology programs have greatly aided in the use of many techniques and analysis without the giant labor of hand calculations. This has been good and bad. Superficial conclusions can be drawn quickly when we use software as we no longer understand how anything is calculated or why there is a proliferation of astrological techniques that are at our fingertips within the software. They can cloud any analysis because there are too many points generated. It becomes difficult to know what are the most important factors to study.

The difficulty is that most of the historical astrological source material are from copies of Greek text that has been transcribed many times from Greek to Persian to Latin. They are in fragments or references to older sources that do not exist. To only base traditional astrology on old texts is a mistake. I believe that a broader perspective is needed to get to the fundamentals of its beginnings. I have found that my knowledge of astrology has been expanded much more widely when I started reading books in other fields of study like archeoastronomy, ancient history, astronomy and the belief systems of other cultures like the Incas and Mayans.

Way too much credit has been given to the Greeks for mathematical and astronomical discoveries. This is likely because the Greeks left written texts whereas the Egyptians left images that demonstrated the same mathematical principles and understandings. Many of these early Greek writers gave credit to the Egyptians, but the Egyptian writings have been lost in time and our modern historians mostly honor the Greeks. For example, Archimedes is credited with discovering the mathematical *pi* but the Egyptians already knew this concept. The one historian that has given greater credit to the Egyptians was Dr. Livio Catullo Stecchini. He was an historian of ancient mathematics and measurements. It was quite clear in his appendix in *The Secrets of the Great Pyramid*, that he discredited the Greeks as discoverers of major mathematical principles but they were students taught by the Egyptians and that the Greeks misunderstood some concepts.[3]

> "Stecchini's evidence shows that far from being the great innovators of geographical knowledge, the Alexandrine geographers of the next half millennium, such as Eratosthenes, Hipparchus and Ptolemy were **mainly handling and mishandling traditional data of an advanced science that preceded them, and which they only understood in part.**"[4]

This is no small matter for astrology because it was the Greek Ptolemy who misunderstood the difference between the Midheaven and the Nonagesimal (the Equal House 10th cusp). According to Stecchini, the Egyptians clearly knew the difference between the Geographic North Pole and the Ecliptic North Pole.[5] The Geographic

North Pole is used to measure the Midheaven and the Ecliptic North Pole is used to measure the Nonagesimal. Ptolemy got these measurements mixed up. This misunderstanding has plagued astrology for a very long time. Now modern astrologers no longer hand calculate horoscopes, so they never learn the measurements of house points or how they are calculated. They don't need to do the math anymore. Most modern astrologers no longer understand these measurement differences.

The basis of Hellenistic planetary order has an astronomical basis but the Greek writers never mentioned it. Astronomy supports the assignment of planets to signs discussed in the chapter of Hellenistic Planetary Order. This is why it is so important for astrologers to study archeoastronomy and ancient history beyond just studying new translations of astrological texts by Greeks or Arabs. Currently in 2014, it is a common theory among astrologers that the zodiac signs were created by the Babylonians and that Hellenistic Egyptians (Greeks living in Egypt) created horoscopic astrology. Yes, the first written horoscopes (100CE) are of that time period, but there is new research that point to Egypt using the zodiac signs before Alexander the Great conquered Egypt, i.e. The Hellenistic Greeks. In 2012 the discovery of an astrologer's board in Croatia has been radiocarbon dated back to 2,200 years ago. An astrologer's board was a horoscope carved in wood and ivory with the signs of the zodiac and slots to move planets and Ascendant around a circle to draw a horoscope. It could be used many times over to cast many charts. These boards could have been used much earlier than the first horoscope found on papyrus paper or clay.[6] Let us remember that early horoscopes were written in tabular form and sometimes drawn in a rectangular form also. They were and still are horoscopes. These rectangular horoscopes are found in the Temple of Dendera and date back to a time older than the last rebuilding of that Temple.

In the Chapter on Precession, there is an image of Aries and Taurus marking the Ages. It was speculated by Robert Bauval in *The Orion Mystery* that the Egyptians marked the Age of Leo with the Head of the Sphinx as a Lion for Leo and that they unified Upper and Lower Egypt after the Age of Gemini when the constellation Orion raised up in declination from precession. These zodiacal signs have been used for a very long period of time. Currently, at Gödekli Tepe, an archeological dig in Turkey is being dated to the ninth millennium BCE. It has two stone pillars carved with lions on the inner faces. These two pillars are aligned east-west to measure the solstice when Leo was rising with the Sun.[7] The Age of Leo may point to the global myths of a great flood that nearly destroyed life on Earth. Scientists have now firmly dated a global catastrophe to ca. 10,900-10,800, the boundary known as the Younger Dryas horizon (possibly caused by a comet) that may be the source of the myth.

These are only traces left behind but they point to an older knowledge base that goes back before the Hellenistic Greeks. There is astrological knowledge in the images left behind in the ancient world that give us the clues to astrology's structure and design. These astronomical and geometric clues can clarify astrology's structure. It can point to a better understanding of its foundations. It can help clear up the ongoing debates of sign and house rulerships that I discuss in this book. It is my hope that these insights can help with the formation of a solid foundation of astrology in the 21st century.

Footnotes

1. http://en.wikipedia.org/wiki/Theosophical_Society
2. Holden, James H., Section on Fifth Period Modern Astrology, *A History of Horoscopic Astrology*, American Federation of Astrology, 2006, p.193-239.
3. Stecchini, Livio Catullo, Appendix of Notes on the Relation of Ancient Measures to the Great Pyramid, *Secrets of The Great Pyramid*, 1971, Harper and Row, New York, p. 287-382.
4. Ibid, p.215.
5. Ibid, p 174.
6. http://news.discovery.com/history/art-history/astrology-board-found-120117.htm
7. Collins, Andrew, Gödekli Tepe, *Genesis of the Gods*, Bear and Company Vermont 2014, p. 4-5.

Astrology as Geometry

There are many ways to approach the foundations of astrology but the most satisfying to me (and to some of our historical 20th century astrologers too) is the recognition that there is an abstract design to astrology's structure. It is built following mathematical principals that were known from its origins and then modern knowledge has added to its complexity. The fundamental statement of "As Above, So Below" is a statement of the microcosm reflecting the same principals as the macrocosm. It was Tons Brunés belief, in his book, *The Secrets of Ancient Geometry*, that mathematics and the alphabet sprang from geometry, not the reverse. He believed the Egyptians used a system of counting that was based on geometric factors; they measured by proportions and ratios

Number and Angles have Quality, just as Time has Quality. They express the principle of energy or process by their very nature. This concept of Number is no longer taught in our school systems since there is a current belief that their numerical value is the only thing worth teaching to the general public. Astrology is a sympathetic study of this concept of Quality regarding Time and Angle. We are dealing with archetypes in astrology that show fundamental patterns that we can identify with events that occur around us and with personality qualities of an individual. The ancient Greeks studied the Quadrivium of geometry or arithmetic, with music and harmony and astronomy with astrology. Robert Lawlor in his book on *Sacred Geometry* omits the astrology since the academic world avoids the word but it was the astrology that made the study of the stars important to the Greeks. To get a deeper understanding of astrology, the study of sacred geometry with the esoteric side of Number can give a greater comprehension of how its principles function in action. This helps to discern the difference between astrological techniques that work or may have an inherent problem in their structure. Lawlor states:

> "...the archetypal is concerned with universal processes or dynamic patterns which can be considered independently of any structure or material form... Ancient cultures symbolized these pure, eternal processes as gods, that is, powers or lines of action through which Spirit is concretized into energy and matter...through the function of leverage; the principle

that ***energies are controlled, specified and modified through the effects of angulation.***

Thus we find that often the angle—which is fundamentally a relationship of two numbers...We find, for example, that a 60° angle has quite different structural and energetic properties from an angle of 90° or of 45°. Likewise, geometric optics reveals that each substance characteristically refracts light at its own particular angle, and it is this angle which gives us our most precise definition of the substance. Furthermore, the angles in the bonding patterns of molecules determine to a great extent the qualities of the substance"[1]

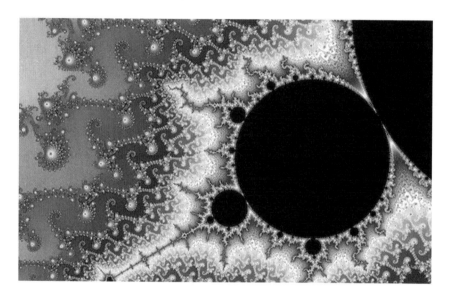

The Mandelbrot Fractal

This is fully expressed in fractal geometry but this modern form of mathematics was only discovered in 1979 by Benoît B. Mandelbrot[2], a mathematician who used IBM computers to calculate sets of numbers that modeled the real world of tree branching, stock market prices, rugged coastlines, the shape of mountain ranges, and the cluster of galaxies and the structure of blood vessels. This is now being used to generate CGI graphics for movie backgrounds like Star Wars. The antenna in cell phones uses this fractal geometry for its design. There is a wonderful NOVA documentary showing fractal geometry in nature and modern applications that demonstrates that many parts of matter and life follow fractal geometry.[3]

Geometry does not imply causal action. Math is a reflection of the real world that can be expressed in the abstract. Astrology is exactly the same. The concepts in fractal geometry are a very close reflection on how astrology was designed and structured. Just as most of living life is built and structured on fractal geometry, astrology is too. It took a very modern mathematician to discover this design because it was too difficult to achieve until a computer could make the laborious calculations. But just like Einstein and Tesla, Mandelbrot saw the design in his mind first. The computer was only an aid to a concept he saw in his mind. Fractals are self-similar, it's one thing repeated over and over just as the human body is a fractal structure repeated over and over.

Geometry and astrology both express life on Earth as an abstract principal. A theorem like the Pythagoras Theorem describes the nature of right triangles as $A^2 + B^2 = C^2$. It does not cause right triangles to behave in a certain way. Any size of right triangles will follow this form and this theorem describes its relationship of the sides to each other. There is also the possibility that astrology could be explained with harmonics but that is just a guess on my part. Science is still in its infancy and there are many subtleties that cannot be measured or tested yet.

With natal astrology it is the assumption that chart patterns at birth describe personality from birth that carry forward for a lifetime. This implies that some form of imprinting goes on at birth. These ideas have not been verified but it is an observation that I believe applies. Is this due to harmonics of vibration or energy? It is just unknown at this time. Astrology is not causal but it is a branch of Euclidian or fractal geometry applied to living matter on Earth. Robert Lawlor states in his book on *Sacred Geometry*:

> "In science today, we are witnessing a general shift away from the assumption that the fundamental nature of matter can be considered from the point of view of substance (particles, quanta) to the concept that the fundamental nature of the material world is knowable only through its underlying patterns of wave forms... The science of musical harmony is in these terms, practically identical with the science of symmetry in crystals...The point of view of modern force-field theory and wave mechanics corresponds to the ancient geometric-harmonic vision of universal order as being an interwoven configuration of wave patterns...The helix [DNA structure] which is a special type from the group

of regular spirals, results from sets of fixed geometric proportions... These proportions can be understood to exist *a priori*, without any material counterpart, as abstract, geometric relationships. The architecture of bodily existence is determined by an invisible, immaterial world of pure form and geometry...Plants, for example, can carry out the process of photosynthesis only because the carbon, hydrogen, nitrogen and magnesium of the chlorophyll molecule are arranged in a complex twelvefold symmetrical pattern, rather like that of a daisy...In mythological thought, twelve most often occurs as the number of the universal mother of life, and so this twelvefold symbol is precise even to the molecular level...Our different perceptual faculties such as sight, hearing, touch and smell are a result then of various proportioned reductions of one vast spectrum of vibratory frequencies. We can understand these proportional relationships as a sort of geometry of perception...The content of our experience results from an immaterial, abstract, geometric architecture which is composed of harmonic waves of energy, nodes of relationality, melodic forms springing forth from the eternal realm of geometric proportion."[4]

Let's take a look at the Quality of Number because astrology uses Number and Angle in its esoteric sense. The ancients always started with One, there was no concept of zero in the ancient world, yet all whole numbers could be generated from One, therefore it's association with God. The closest use of One in astrology is the conjunction aspect of zero degree. The conjunction of o degree is strongly associated with the Sun. As Number is discussed next, please remember that Number and Angle are both represented.

One and Unity

First there was the One, God, the undivided All, the Word, or Om. A circle or a dot generally represents this. The Japanese showed Creation formed geometrically. (see top of the next page) Read from right to the left, first there is a circle transformed into a triangle which is transformed into a square, to represent the manifestation of the World.

Japanese Zen Calligraphy of Creation

Here is the image of the Sound of Om, or it could be said, in the beginning was the Word, or it started with the Big Bang, which looks very similar to this image of electronic beam frequency interference patterns: The footnote is to an excellent video on vibration patterns[5]:

The Sound of Om

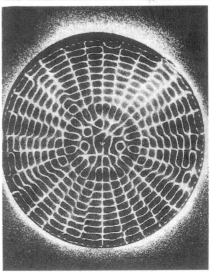

**Vibratory Patterns
of Sound Frequencies**

It's interesting to note that the world class inventor, Nicolas Tesla said: "If you want to find the secrets of the universe, think in terms of energy, frequency and vibration."

Two as Duality and Transformation into Multiplicity

The ancient world did not have the concept of zero. Everything started with One. And it was understood that One could generate all the other whole numbers from itself. Below is a square with each side equal to one unit. The diagonal of the square, which is √2 can generate the next square that has a side of 2, then 3, then 4, etc. It is the *generative power* of the square root of two that creates multiplicity.

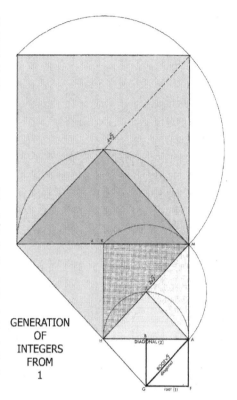

GENERATION OF INTEGERS FROM 1

The Generation of Whole Numbers from One, from the One Comes the Many

The square root of Two has generative qualities. Its the principle of alternation that is seen in cell division and root generation and the image of Yin and Yang. Lawlor states:

> "The diagonal of the square will always be an 'incommensurable', 'irrational' number of decimal places without ever arriving at a resolution. In the case of the diagonal of the square, this decimal is 1.4142... and is called the square root of 2, or √2. With the circle,..the circumference will also always be of the incommensurable type, 3.12159...which we know by the Greek symbol π, *pi*...The square root of 2 is the functional number of a square. *Pi* is the functional number of a circle... The irrational functions are a key opening a door to a higher reality of Number. They

demonstrate that Number is above all a relationship; and no matter what quantities are applied to the side and to the diameter the relationship will remain invariable, for in essence this functional aspect of Number is neither large nor small, neither infinite or finite, it is universal. Thus within the concept of Number there is a definite, finite, particularizing power and also a universal synthesizing power. One may be called the exoteric or external aspect of number, the other is the esoteric or inner, functional aspect."[6]

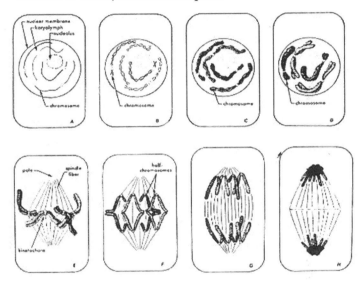

Cell Division from One to the Many

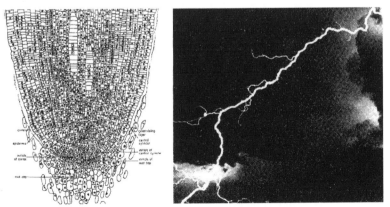

**Root Growth and Lighting as a
Function of Alternation of Two and √2**

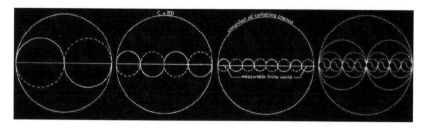

Yin and Yang as a Principle of Alternation

In astrology we can divide the signs into the Principle of Duality, representing Two, Opposites or Alternation. This is used with the opposition aspect of 180 degrees. The ancient terms were Masculine and Feminine. But astrology deals with Time. Another word for this duality is Past and Future. A chart is basically a moment in Time representing the balance of the Past and the Future. This ordering is based on Tobey's Mate Signs of Polarity.[7]

Past Signs	Rulers	Future Signs
Cancer	Moon/Sun	Leo
Virgo	Mercury/?	Gemini
Taurus	?/Venus	Libra
Scorpio	Mars/Pluto	Aries
Pisces	Neptune/Jupiter	Sagittarius
Capricorn	Saturn/Uranus	Aquarius

Or this order:

Past Signs		
Cancer	opposes	Capricorn
Scorpio	opposes	Taurus
Pisces	opposes	Virgo
Future Signs		
Leo	opposes	Aquarius
Aries	opposes	Libra
Sagittarius	opposes	Gemini

The signs of the zodiac are carefully arranged to alternate the Past against the Future signs by mate signs of polarity and by alternation:

Cancer	Past
Leo	Future
Virgo	Past
Libra	Future
Scorpio	Past
Sagittarius	Future
Capricorn	Past
Aquarius	Future
Pisces	Past
Aries	Future
Taurus	Past
Gemini	Future

The zodiac follows a pattern of duality by both co-rulership and by opposition:

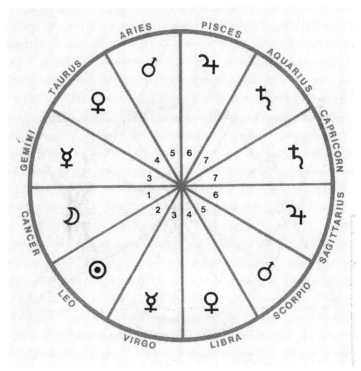

Zodiac Signs with Ancient Co-Rulers

This Power of Generation by the duality of the opposites is expressed strongly in astrology. In modern terms we divide aspects between two main categories of Hard Aspects that are in 30 degree divisions of 0, 90, and 180 degrees. They are said to be the strongest of aspects and the most likely to produce events. The Soft Aspects are the 30-degree divisions of 60 and 120. They are said to represent the creative and fortunate events. When the strength of houses is analyzed, the 1st, 4th, 7th and 10th are considered the most important. They represent the division of houses by 2 and 2^2.

Three and the Power of Formation

Another way to divide the circle is into Three. With three points, a surface can be created.

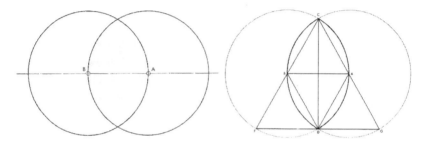

<table>
<tr><td align="center">**The intersecting circles form a Vesica Piscis that generates $\sqrt{3}$**</td><td align="center">**The Jointing of Heaven and Earth (two circles) Generating the $\sqrt{3}$ and therefore Creation**</td></tr>
</table>

The Vesica Piscis and the $\sqrt{3}$ create a union between Heaven and Earth, yin and yang, or past and future to produce form or the trinity. It is from $\sqrt{2}$ that divides a square into many and the $\sqrt{3}$ divides the volume-form of a cube. Hence the trinity is the creative basis of all form. The Vesica generates all polygons. It is a creative force and synonymous with Spirit. It can be viewed as the balancing of the opposites (following page):

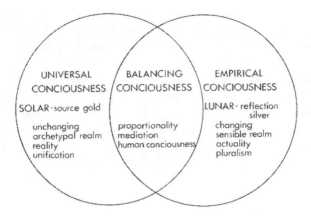

UNIVERSAL CONCIOUSNESS

SOLAR · source gold

unchanging
archetypal realm
reality
unification

BALANCING CONCIOUSNESS

proportionality
mediation
human conciousness

EMPIRICAL CONCIOUSNESS

LUNAR · reflection
silver

changing
sensible realm
actuality
pluralism

Intelligence is the Mediator Between Two Realms

This concept was used extensively in Christianity in the symbol of the Fish and the Age of Pisces to represent the generative spirit of the trinity. Christ is inside the Vesica as the generative, spiritual force of creation. He is one with the Holy Spirit and God as he forms the Trinity and he is then surrounded by the images of rulership of the Piscean Age.

Christ inside the Vesica with Four Apostles in the Fixed Cross of Scorpio, Aquarius, Taurus and Leo denoting Kingship

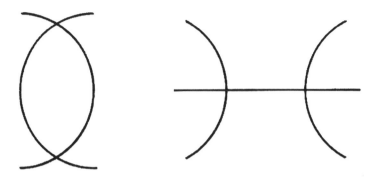

**The Vesica forms the Symbol for Pisces
and the Christian Fish**

Astrologically, the zodiac can be divided by 3, which produce the four elements of Water, Earth, Fire and Air. Like the terms masculine and feminine, we can rename these elements to more modern psychological terms that are synonymous with these Elements (to be discussed in another chapter).

Water	opposed by	Earth	All Past Signs
Cancer	opposed by	Capricorn	Individual Survival
Scorpio	opposed by	Taurus	Family Survival
Pisces	opposed by	Virgo	Social Survival
Fire	**opposed by**	**Air**	**All Future Signs**
Leo	opposed by	Aquarius	Individual non-Survival
Aries	opposed by	Libra	Family non-Survival
Sagittarius	opposed by	Gemini	Social non-Survival

These trines within each Element are considered to be the most harmonious of combinations of Water with Water, Earth with Earth, Fire with Fire, or Air with Air since they all form 120-degree aspects between the signs. Since the zodiac has 12 signs, the division by 3 gives 3 signs to 4 elements.

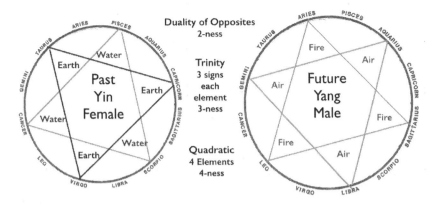

**Duality with the Trinity
and the Quadratic Divisions of the Zodiac**

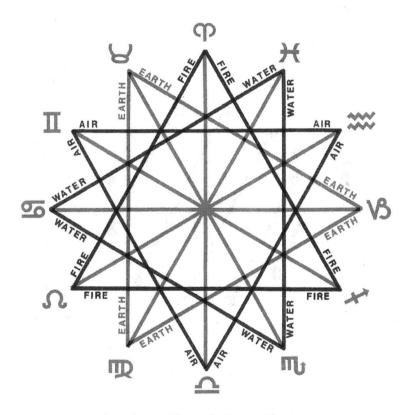

The Three Signs in Four Elements

Four and the Manifest Material World

Four is the square of Two (2x2) so it doesn't have a generative square root like 2 or 3 but it is a product of 2^2 and is the first number that can represent in three dimensions an object in the physical world. This is why the pyramid was so important an object in the ancient world. It represented the principle of One, Two, Three and Four in one form. The apex is One or Unity, a second point down one side is Two or Duality, a third point creates a triangle of Three or Creative, and a forth point creates a base square and an object of three dimensions of Four or the Manifest World.

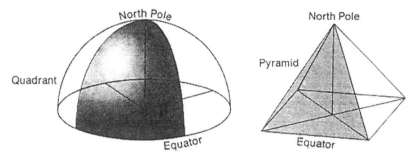

The Great Pyramid, each face representing a Quadrant of the North Hemisphere

Astrologically it creates the three crosses of Cardinal, Fixed and Mutable with four signs in each. Each of the three crosses have signs that are 90 and 180 degrees apart and each have a balance of Past and Future.

Cardinal Cross			Internally Driven	
Cancer	opposed by	Capricorn	Individual Survival	Past
Aries	opposed by	Libra	Family Non-Survival	Future
Fixed Cross			**Stubborn**	
Scorpio	opposed by	Taurus	Family Survival	Past
Leo	opposed by	Aquarius	Individual Non-Survival	Future
Mutable Cross			**Flexible**	
Pisces	opposed by	Virgo	Social Survival	Past
Sagittarius	opposed by	Gemini	Social Non-Survival	Future

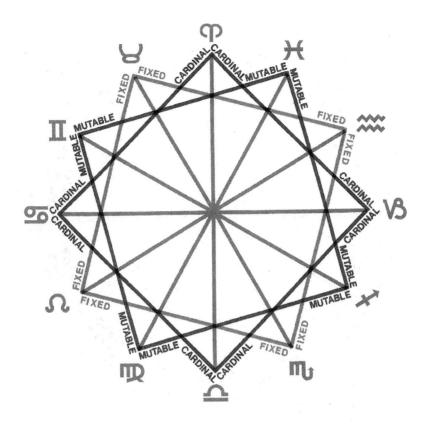

The Cardinal, Fixed, and Mutable Crosses

This creates a final pattern for each sign to have the unique attributes of the duality of past and future; one of four elements or Water, Earth, Fire and Air; and one of three crosses of Cardinal, Fixed or Mutable; which gives each sign a unique characteristic from the others.

Astrology is also about Time and that Time has Quality. Just as in Geometry, Number and Angle have Quality too. In Robert L. Lawlor's book on *Sacred Geometry*, he states:

> Functioning then at the archetypal level, Geometry and number describe fundamental, causal energies in their interwoven, eternal dance. Geometry deals with pure form, and philosophical geometry re-enacts the

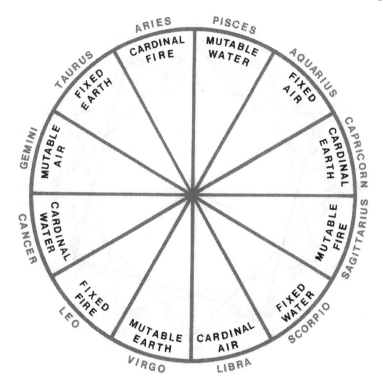

The Completed Twelve Divisions with Each Unique Sign

unfolding of each form out of a preceding one. It is a way by which the essential creative mystery is rendered visible. The passage from creation to procreation from the unmanifest, pure, formal ideas to the 'here-below', the world that spins out from that original divine stroke, can be mapped out by geometry, and experienced through the practice of geometry...Inseparable from this process is the concept of Number...But Number in this context must be understood in a special way. When Pythagoras said 'All is arranged according to Number', he was not thinking of numbers in the ordinary, enumerative sense. In addition to simple *quantity*, numbers on the ideal level are possessed of *quality*, so that 'twoness', 'threeness' or fourness', for example, are not merely composed of 2,3, or 4 units, but are wholes or unities in themselves, each having related powers. 'Two', for instance, is seen as the original essence from which the *power of duality* proceeds and drives its reality.[8]

Wheel pendants dating to the second half of the 2nd millennium BC, found in Zürich, are held at the Swiss National Museum. Commonly they are shown with just a cross for four seasons but the center makes Five. Variants include a six-spoke wheel, a central empty circle, and a second circle with twelve spokes surrounding one of four spokes.[9]

The numbers One, Two, Three, and Four are the fundamental numbers that astrology uses to divide a circle of 360 degrees but the numbers 5, 7, 9, 12 and 13 are very important too. Chinese astrology utilizes five elements but Western only uses four. Yet Five is a very important number in sacred geometry and in fractals. Five is implied in Western astrology by the crossed circle that represents the solstices and equinoxes. The center point of the circle is the 5th point.

Five, the Square Root of $\sqrt{5}$, Phi or Φ

Pythagoras is given credit for discovering the transcendent ratio of *Phi* but more recent work shows that this proportion was well know to the Egyptians as it was embedded into the Great Pyramid and other structures.

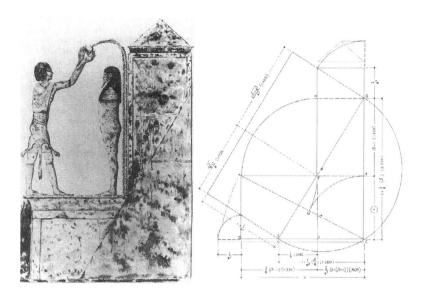

The Tomb of Petosiris was built around 300 BC in the Ptolemaic period. All the priests in the Petosiris family bore the title of 'Great of the Five' and 'Master of the Seat'.

The Hidden Sacred Geometry within the Throne's Design

The Golden Mean of *Phi* was embedded within Egyptian images and structures for only 'One Who Has The Eye To See' could get the hidden message within the design. Knowledge was not shared freely, membership in the priesthood was required and sharing knowledge with others was forbidden by pain of death. It was in Greek architecture, Leonard de Vinci called it 'The Divine Proportion' and Leonardo Fibonacci discovered it as a number series that describes body proportions and tree branching distribution. *Phi* continues to open new doors in our understanding of life and the universe. It appeared in Roger Penrose's discovery in the 1970's of "**Penrose Tiles**," which first allowed surfaces to be tiled in five-fold symmetry. Mandelbrot used it for Fractal Geometry and it appeared again in the 1980's in **quasi-crystals**, a newly discovered form of matter.[10]

Fibonacci Chamomile   Wiki Commons CC BY 2.5

Cell Division and Fractal Geometry

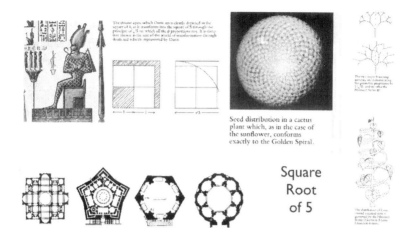

Seed distribution in a cactus
plant which, as in the case of
the sunflower, conforms
exactly to the Golden Spiral.

Square Root of 5

The Creative Power of Five and √5

Egyptian king as the hypothe-
nuse of a sacred 3–4–5 triangle formed by a snake.
Schwaller de Lubicz shows
the king as φ², split into a
φ + 1 proportion by the
phallus. The king's raised arm
gives a 6/5, or 1.2 × φ²,
proportion, which is exactly
3.1416, or π.

Pythagoras: 'All is arranged
according to Number'
Numbers on the ideal level
are possessed of Quality
so that 2-ness, 3-ness
or 4-ness are Unities
in themselves having powers.

* 2.618 × 6/5 = 3.1416.

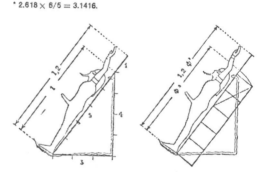

The Pharaoh shown as The Generative Power of √5

Dividing a circle by Five gives angles of 72 and 36 degrees. These are considered minor aspects in astrology but there could be new discoveries with these angles that are not identified yet. Five does relate to the Seven visible planets of Moon, Sun, Mercury, Venus, Mars, Jupiter and Saturn versus the Five possible Invisible planets of which three have been discovered as Uranus, Neptune and Pluto (classified now as a Planetoid). Now Eris (discovered in 2005) is a possible astrological ruler since it is just as big as Pluto. Is there one more to complete the pattern of Twelve?

Six is a minor number since it a multiple of 3 but it is related to duality since it divides the signs in half and the circle in half for the opposition aspect of 180 degrees.

Seven for seven visible planets, seven Chakras, seven white piano keys with five black keys, the seven-fold path, the fourth Prime number, seven days, 7 notes in a scale, seven deadly sins, the Big Dipper with its seven stars, seven rainbow colors, etc. According to Wikipedia, 7 was considered a God number and the Pharaoh usually ordered things in groups with multiples of 7. For a time, 7 was not even used in writings for the people of Egypt, it was considered to be too sacred.

Eight is a multiple of Four but it is extensively used to mark the midpoint of the seasons so it is common to see a circle with eight divisions. Dividing a circle by Eight does create two more minor Hard Aspects with the 45 degree (half of 90) and the 135 degree (90 + 45). Traditionally these degrees where not used but Kepler popularized them for astrology.

Nine is 3x3 for 3^2 and it is highly related to Precession. Every fraction of Precession will add up to Nine so it is strongly associated with Gaia or Mother Earth.

Precessional Fractions
Gaia, Earth Goddess

25,920	= 2+5+9+2+0	= 1+8	= 9 full cycle
12,960	= 1+2+9+6+0	= 1+8	= 9 half cycle
4,320	= 4+3+2+0		= 9 1/6th or 2 ages
2,160	= 2+1+6+0		= 9 one age or sign
1,080	= 1+0+8+0		= 9 half of an age
540	= 5+4+0		= 9 quarter of an age (same as a Jupiter/Saturn cycle)
432	= 4+3+2		= 9 fifth of a age
360	= 3+6+0		= 9 five degrees
108	= 1+0+8		= 9 one and a half degrees
72	= 7+2		= 9 one degree
36	= 3+6		= 9 half of a degree

Gaia Number Nine as a Fraction of Precession

Buddha had the nine virtues, Ramadan is in the ninth lunar month, the Chinese Dragon is associated with nine, and pregnancy is nine months. The Persians associate Nine with Jupiter and Good Fortune. The Ninth astrological house is considered fortunate and ruled by Jupiter.

Recently, Russell Ohlhausen has found that the Fibonacci Numbers can all be reduced to the number 9 and that they can be matched to the zodiac signs starting with Cancer. This pattern follows Hellenistic Planetary Order so this is another correspondence of geometry design in the zodiac.

**The Sri Yantra with Nine Triangles,
Four Down and Five Up[12]**

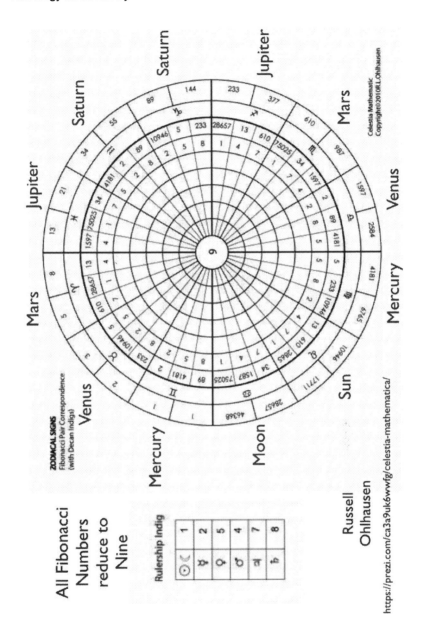

**Fibonacci Numbers matched to Zodiac
and Hellenistic Planetary Order[11]**

Ten is a multiple of 5 x 2. Ten fingers and toes, the decimal system, ten plagues of Egypt, the Ten Stems in Chinese astrology, the ten Sephirot in the Kabbala

Eleven is a Master number in Numerology and a Prime number, the Sunspot cycle is 11 years.

Twelve is the combination of 3 and 4, 5 and 7 and 12 is the most popular division of a circle in astrology which represent the solar months of the year and 24 hours in a day (12x2). There are endless references to 12 in most religions, 12 inches in a foot.

Thirteen has gotten a modern negative attitude since the current patriarchal religions have put down the old goddess religions that honored the lunar months of 13 in a solar year. The oldest forms of astrology were lunar based which is still maintained in Jyotish astrology. A boy becomes a man in Judaism at Thirteen, the Twelve Disciples plus Jesus made Thirteen, it represents the Feminine and the menstrual cycle, again lunar, Thirteen colonies started the USA which is a high Masonic number for the Thirteen Secrets.

There are many patterns and complexities with Numbers but this list is sufficient from an astrological perspective. Sacred geometry can be a rich source of information to guide the search of hidden patterns in astrology that is embedded in its design and structure.

Footnotes

1. Lawlor, Robert L., *Sacred Geometry*, Thames & Hudson, London 1982, p. 6-8.
2. http://en.wikipedia.org/wiki/Benoit_Mandelbrot
3. https://www.youtube.com/watch?v=lmxJiKDR_s0   Hunting the Hidden Dimension by NOVA
4. Lawlor, p. 4-5.
5. A great video on geometric sound patterns, https://www.youtube.com/watch?v=wvJAgrUBF4w
6. Lawlor, p. 11-12.
7. Tobey, Carl Payne, *Collected Works of Carl Payne Tobey*, Bonami Inc, Texas 1998, p. 59.
8. Lawlor, p. 10-11.
   Lawlor, p. 12-13 states:
   "Let us look at the first four primary numbers in this spirit.
   The number One can of course define a quantity; as for example, one apple. But in its other sense, it perfectly represents the principle of absolute unity, and as such has often been used as the symbol to represent God. As a statement of form it can in one sense represent a point – it has been called the 'pointal' number, the *bindu* or seed in the Hindu mandala—or in another sense it can represent the perfect circle.

Two is a quantity, but symbolically it represents, as we have already seen, the principle of Duality, the power of multiplicity. At the same time it has its formal sense in the presentation of a line, in that two points define a line.

Three is a quantity, but as a principle it represent the Trinity in its formal sense is that of the triangle. Which is formed from three points. With three a qualitative transition is made from the pure abstract elements of point and line to the tangible, measurable state which is called a *surface*. In India the triangle was called the Mother, for it is the membrane or birth channel through which all the transcendent powers of unity and its initial division into polarity must pass in order to enter into the manifest realm of surface. The triangle acts as the mother of form.

But three is yet only a principle of creation, forming the passage between the transcendent and the manifest realms, whereas Four represent at last the 'first born thing', the world of Nature, because it is the product of the procreative process, that is of multiplication: $2 \times 2 = 4$. As a form, four is the square, and represents materialization.

The universality of Number can be seen in another, more physical context. We learn from modern physics that from gravity to electromagnetism, light, heat, and even in what we think of as solid matter itself, the entire perceptible universe is composed of vibrations, perceived by us as wave phenomena. Waves are pure temporal patterns, that is dynamic configurations composed of amplitude, interval and frequency, and they can be defined and understood by us only through Number. Thus our whole universe is reducible to Number. Every living body physically vibrates, all elemental or inanimate matter vibrates molecularly or atomically, and every vibrating body emits a sound. The study of sound, as the ancients intuited, provides a key to the understanding of the universe."

9.   Wikipedia image by Radanhaenger-edited
11. https://prezi.com/ca3a9uk6wwfg/celestia-mathematica/
12. Wikipedia SriYantra constructCC BY-SA 3.0

Sign Rulership with Hellenistic Planetary Order

It is well known that the Egyptians started their solar year at 0 Cancer, the summer solstice. This was the time of the annual flooding of the Nile, the reappearance of Sirius, the star of Isis and the season to plant crops. They made the southern boundary of Egypt fall on the exact position of the Tropic of Cancer on the first Cataract of the Nile and then they extended the north boundary of Egypt exactly 7 degrees latitude because Mercury had the most extreme latitude of the visible planets. Mercury defined the width of the zodiac belt to be a total of 14 degrees and they associated Mercury as the God of Measurement[1] and also Thoth.

The sign of Cancer was very important to the Egyptians and they assigned the Moon as its ruler. The next sign of Leo was given to the Sun, then the assignment of Mercury to Virgo, Venus to Libra, and Mars to Scorpio, etc. This drove me crazy in my first studies back in the 1960's. Why, why did they give the planetary order as Moon, Sun, Mercury, Venus, Mars, etc.? Any basic education given in elementary school shows us the solar system in the order of Sun, Mercury, Venus, Earth, Mars, etc. Were they stupid and didn't know any better? It's impossible for the Sun to be closer to the Earth than Venus or Mercury!

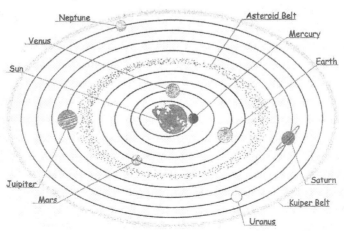

Heliocentric Solar System

The Egyptians had studied the skies for more than 4,000 years. How could they get this so wrong? They were obsessed with the sky and creating Heaven on Earth. They knew the circumference of the Earth and that the Earth flatten at the poles! The Great Pyramid is aligned exactly to the cardinal directions. Only modern instruments can get as exact as the Egyptians did in the Age of Taurus! What is wrong with this picture?

In 1992 I began a quest to confirm astrological theories that I had been taught, find their actual basis and verify the proof. In the 1990s, I acquired over 200 publications seeking this documentation through interlibrary loans. I took multiple trips to Europe to look at Egyptian artifacts while searching for these clues. My search lead me to London to the British Museum, to Paris to the Louvre and to Egypt to Esna, Luxor, Dendera and Cairo. In the course of 20 years of research, some of my best discoveries were not found in astrological texts but in other fields like archeoastronomy, ancient mathematics and history. Luck, timing and synchronicity all played their part in piecing the puzzle together. Finally I think I now have enough verification to write about the first of these missing elements to help the advancement of astrology in this new century. Ancient co-rulerships were:

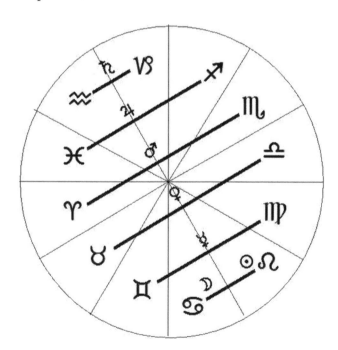

Classic Hellenistic sign and planet rulership

Cancer and Leo are the only signs solely assigned to a single luminary of the Moon and Sun respectively. Then the co-rulership signs go in order of Virgo-Gemini ruled by Mercury, Libra-Taurus ruled by Venus, Scorpio-Aries ruled by Mars, Sagittarius-Pisces ruled by Jupiter, and finally Capricorn-Aquarius ruled by Saturn.

The first big stroke of luck for my research came at the Louvre in 1993. In the bookstore was a copy of the magazine, *Archeologia*[2] with a picture of the Egyptian Sky Goddess Nut on the cover. She had the signs of the zodiac running down both sides of her body in the co-rulership order. It was from the Hellenistic Egyptian period of 200 AD.[3] There are at least three of these images documented in various museums. Inside the lid of the sarcophagus was the planetary order that I had been looking for. **The order is very important**. It starts with the two luminary signs of Cancer and Leo on opposite sides of her body. Cancer and Leo have single rulers of the Moon and Sun. Then the co-rulership signs extend down Nut's body as Gemini and Virgo co-ruled by Mercury, Taurus and Libra, co-ruled by Venus, Aries and Scorpio co-ruled by Mars, Pisces and Sagittarius co-ruled by Jupiter, Aquarius and Capricorn co-ruled by Saturn.

Goddess Nut from 200 A.D.

In 1996 I was at the Project Hindsight Conference in Ithaca, NY lead by Robert Hand and Robert Schmidt on Hellenistic Astrology. The large room was full of astrologers and anonymous academics from Cornell University. During lunch, I had a conversation with Avery Solomon who had a Ph.D. in Mathematics and taught at Cornell University. I shared with him that Carl Payne Tobey had claimed that the planetary order assigned to zodiacal signs was based on the average mean distance from the Earth. Avery had the necessary software on his PC to model the principle of celestial mechanics. He showed me that from the Earth's point of view, Mercury and Venus did stay behind the Sun the majority of the time. The model confirmed the Hellenistic planetary order. Sadly I didn't get a copy of his program. I saw the proof but I didn't have the solid evidence.

The Roman Catholic Cathedral of Vezelay
Zodiac Signs Divided Between Cancer-Leo

Yet with the discoveries in the Western World by Kepler of planetary motion and Galileo's re-discovery of the Sun as the center of the Solar System, why did this strange astrological order persist? The Roman Catholic Cathedral of Vezelay, France still displays the old planetary order but with Christ in the center, rather than the Goddess Nut dividing the signs between Cancer and Leo.

The Ancient World believed in keeping knowledge secret so that rulers and priests could maintain power. Many truths and knowledge were recorded in picture form. You had to have enough learning to understand the messages left behind. Most of the mathematical and astronomical discoveries we attribute to the Hellenistic Greeks were already known in Egypt. They were the great geometric experts in the Ancient World. The Greeks gained their knowledge from what was left of the Egyptian priesthood. This is well documented by an expert in ancient measurements, Dr. Livio Stecchini.[4] The Egyptians already knew about precession, Pi, Phi, the Golden Mean, right triangles, the Fibonacci numbers and a form of calculus (later discovered by Newton). They did this with geometry and ratios, long before Arabic numbers or algebra (a form of mathematical notation).[5]

But much was lost with the conquests of Egypt. We only have pieces and hints of this knowledge through monuments, objects and fragments of texts that have been translated multiple times. The libraries at Heliopolis were destroyed. The rulers and priests were killed so that the conquerors could control the population. First there was the Persian Conquest of 525 BC and then Alexander the Great's conquest of Egypt in 330 BC. Nick Campion points out that there is a 600-year void of astrological writings after the Fall of Rome in 476 AD. Hellenistic Greek astrology was preserved by the Arabs and transmitted to Europe during the Arab occupation of southern Spain. This was the start of the Renaissance, the foundation of medieval astrology and our recovery of Hellenistic astrology.

As astrologers, we have forgotten to look at the astronomy side of this picture for the answers. All of our astrological structure is based on sacred geometry, astronomy and mathematics. The best minds in the Ancient World were astrologers until the Church and the Scientific Revolution (1750 to 1850 AD) suppressed astrology. We are still recovering this knowledge thanks to serious scholars like Robert Zoller, Robert Hand, Robert Schmidt and Benjamin Dykes in reconstructing our past with new translations. Now we have a new generation of young astrologers trying to put the pieces together like Chris Brennan and others. Add to this the power of computing and the Internet to disperse this reconstructed knowledge, we can now share this revived knowledge with our colleagues in India and the Arab World. There is said to be over a million astrological manuscripts to be translated in India, let alone the Arab World and in China.

However, the fundamental issue of planetary order has yet to be explained. Carl Payne Tobey discovered this answer

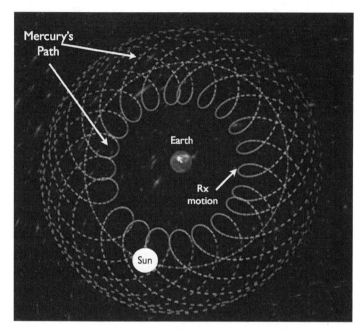

Mercury and the Sun traveling around Geocentric Earth

back in the 1933. This is because he studied the sacred geometry structure embedded in astrology's design. But he left no proof and no references. It simply wasn't the style of astrologers in the early to mid 20th century to document. A good portion of what they discovered for themselves was shared with their private students but not necessarily published. We can thank James H. Holden for documenting 2,200 astrologer profiles[6] and to the few astrological libraries we have in the USA and UK that have preserved 20th century manuscripts so we can recall the work of past astrologers in the prior century.

The image above a screen shot of John Mick's video on the geocentric model of the Sun and Mercury traveling around the Earth.[7] He used the real position and velocity data from NASA/JPL. This is a video on YouTube that I highly recommend watching. The Earth is at the center. The Sun is a small dot going around the Earth in a single circle. The rest of all the curved lines are many years of Mercury transits from the Earth's point of view. The key element is that most of Mercury's transit time is outside the Sun's circle. Mercury spends more time behind the Sun from the viewpoint of Earth. The loops are Mercury stations and retrograde periods.

The image on the next page is a screen shot from John Mick's video of the Sun and Venus traveling around the Earth.[8] The Earth is in the center of both images. The Sun is a small dot

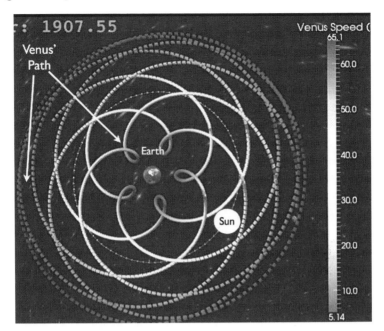

Venus and the Sun traveling around Geocentric Earth

in a single circle around the Earth. All the outer circles are either Mercury or Venus moving around the Earth over a period of years. It is very clear in both images that Mercury and Venus spend more time on the far side of the Sun. **The Sun is closer to Earth during most times of the year than Mercury or Venus.** When the inner planets of Mercury and Venus cross in front of the Sun's path they slow down and then appear to us as being in retrograde motion. This is the proof that these ancient astrologers knew that the Sun is closest to the Earth, after the Moon, most of the time. They weren't so stupid after all. **They knew about average mean distance!** Think about it. If the Egyptians observed Venus as a morning and evening star for hundreds or thousands of years, it's likely they figured it out that Venus was moving behind the Sun. For example, the base of the Great Pyramid is a ratio of the circumference of the Earth and each face represents a quarter of the Northern Hemisphere. **I believe the Egyptians knew these facts and showed it in picture form with the Sky Goddess Nut.**

This planetary assignment follows a system of logic based on an observable astronomical fact of average mean distance to the Earth. It brings us to the discovery of the outer planets of Uranus, Neptune and Pluto. If we maintain this planetary order of average mean distance, then Uranus must be assigned to Aquarius, Neptune to Pisces and Pluto to Aries. This is not a haphazard assignment done by wishful thinking. **This is beyond coincidence.**

Carl Tobey discovered this key observation in 1933 and published it in 1938 and 1954. Concerning the modern rulership of sign assignment to planets by average mean distance, Carl deduced:

> "If we agree to identify the Moon with the zodiacal sign Cancer, then the accepted system of rulership around the zodiac from Cancer to Pisces [Moon thru Neptune] in a counter-clockwise direction follows an arithmetical pattern. It coincides with the mean distance of each body from the earth. Since the [modern] astrologers did not consider mean distance in associating the planets with the various zodiacal signs, the probability of this pattern conforming with mean distance may be expressed as follows:
>
> $$\frac{1}{11 \times 10 \times 9 \times 8 \times 7 \times 6 \times 5 \times 4} = \frac{1}{6,652,800}$$
>
> Thus, the odds in favor of mean distance from the earth being the factor that determines what the ancients called 'rulership' of the planets over the zodiacal signs are **6,652,799 to 1**. From this mathematical point of view alone, Pluto, being the first planet beyond Neptune, must coincide with Aries. Its nature must be that of Aries."[9]

As a minor side note, please remember that one of the original meanings of the word 'rulership' is 'to rule' or 'ruler' also meant to measure or to measure lengths. I believe this is the original meaning of rulership in astrology. **It is to measure.** Just like the Egyptians were the master geometers, they made Mercury the God of Measurement!

I understand this stirs up the debate about the assignment of Pluto to Aries but it cannot be avoided.[10] As a student of modern and traditional astrology, I can understand the avoidance of using the outer planets. It upsets the Essential Dignities. The only way to use the Dignities is to use only the old co-rulerships. Using the old rulerships keeps all the Hellenistic and Medieval rules and techniques in place. Jyotish astrologers have the same problem using the outer planets in evaluations. They only use the old co-rulers for the Dignities. But many Jyotish astrologers do incorporate the newly discovered planets for transits. This is the recognition of these three new planets having an astrological effect, but no one wants to deal with updating the Dignities. At least now there is strong evidence that **Average Mean Distance from Earth** is the basis of the underlying pattern behind Hellenistic planetary order.

There is just too much evidence that the outer planets are real and they work. At some point these conflicting issues need to be addressed. Having Uranus on the Ascendant in a natal chart is not the same as having Saturn there by substitution to conform to the Dignities. Having Jupiter be the ruler of Pisces is not the same as having Neptune as its ruler. These are poor substitutes considering that we have more than 100 years in studying these planets. This disturbs Receptions when using the newly discovered planets. When the technique of finding final dispositorship is used, it can give a false answer because of only using the old rulerships. Integrated modern astrology needs the Dignities revised. This is necessary in the integration of the traditional and modern astrology for this century.

Footnotes

1. Stecchini, Livio Catullo,"Notes on the Relation of Ancient Measures to the Great Pyramid," Appendix to *Secrets of the Great Pyramid* by Peter Tompkins, Harper and Row 1971, pages 294-5.

2. "Le Zodiaque de Pharaon" by Christiane Desroches-Noblecort, *Archeologia* Numero 292, Juillet-Aout 1993, pages 21-45

3. http://www.britishmuseum.org/explore/highlights/article_index/f/the_family_of_soter.aspx The tomb of the Soter family of Archon of Thebes, discovered in 1820, contained fourteen mummies in rectangular wooden coffins. The coffins belonged to members of the family of Soter, Archon of Thebes. Several of the coffins were inscribed in Greek with Soter's name and genealogy, which means that they can be dated precisely to the early second century AD. Theban Tomb 32 in the el-Khokha area on the west bank of the Nile.

4. Stecchini, Livio Catullo ,"Notes on the Relation of Ancient Measures to the Great Pyramid," Appendix to *Secrets of the Great Pyramid* by Peter Tompkins, Harper and Row 1971, pages 287-382.

5. http://www.metrum.org/measures/index.htm

6. James H. Holden, *Biographical Dictionary of Western Astrologers*, A.F.A., 2013.

7. https://www.youtube.com/watch?v=VhA4bl7B-1M&list=PLEBA7CD7FD2564042&feature=c4-overview-vl Published 28 April 2012.

8. https://www.youtube.com/watch?v=30yPAUkQ4ds&list=PLEBA7CD7FD2564042

9. *Carl Payne Tobey's Collected Works on Astrology*, editor Naomi Bennett 1998, p. 162

10. "Does Pluto Rule Scorpio or Aries?" article by Naomi Bennett 1996, www.learnastrologynow.com

Water and Earth Signs of the Past

The zodiac signs are designed with duality in their very structure. All Water signs are opposed by Earth, they are opposites. And there is a duality of opposites between Water and Earth being balanced or opposed by corresponding Fire and Air. Half of the signs are considered Feminine and half are considered Masculine. As we stated before in a prior chapter since astrology is basically about Time, we can rename the terms Feminine and Masculine to Past and Future.

Dramatic code words like Water had a purpose in the ancient world. They were and are archetypical images that convey more depth of meaning in the most simple of terms or images. Water has no form. The vessel that contains it, like the edge of a lake, the banks of a river or the clay of a pot shapes water. This is water that is contained. But what happens with too much water? It pours over the banks of the river, it flows over the top of a dam, and it wipes out buildings and people in a flood or a hurricane. It can become a torrent that takes everything with it like a tsunami. This is the power of Water and it is the same power of human emotion that can drive behavior out of control. The ancients equated three emotions with Water. It was a good analogy of how emotions can overwhelm and flood a person with the deep compulsion of SURVIVAL.

Survival of the Self	Cancer	Past
Survival of the Family	Scorpio	Past
Survival of the Group	Pisces	Past

There are three types of survival emotions that astrology recognizes, as noted above. The most basic is survival of the self, which is the hunger drive. Will there be enough food to live? This is symbolized with Cancer the Crab that is Cardinal Water, ruled by the Moon and associated with the Breasts and Stomach. Why these body parts? The infant's first food is breast milk from its mother. The stomach receives the food and gives the signal that it's hungry. This is the most fundamental of all emotional drives. Will I have enough to eat? The basis of trade was the exchange of food and items for survival. The ruler of Cancer is the Moon, which is associated with the mother, women, money and how to earn a living, all of which can be associated with survival of the self.

Similarly, money can flow like water; easy come, easy go. They can smell the deal and seek out the bottom line for a trade. The need for security may drive them to marry for money or security. They can never have enough money in the bank and are likely to keep a secret, hidden stash of money for desperate times. Cancerians can get desperate when one doesn't know where the next meal will come from. If unchecked, Cancer can never feel safe and secure. The need to protect themselves from famine can drive them to be very successful business people. If we understand this great need of hunger and survival, many of the Cancerian behaviors can be understood for the deep need or compulsion to accumulate. It is especially important to the Cancerian child to have their security needs met so that the unbridled need to gather more and more can be tamed by their early experience of security and safety. Tobey stated of Cancer in his astrology course:

> "One person may become a thief or a sharp businessman. His methods may ultimately destroy him, but if they do not, they may do ample damage to others. He may be very selfish, and he may overeat, thus ruining his health. There may be balancing factors, so that he gets along without too serious consequences. After all, he is friendly. He is not violent. He is nice to you, and you will have to like him, because he seems harmless. You may feel sorry for him. He is such an inoffensive person. He wants company, for he is insecure. He never likes to be alone. He might marry for money. He has a close affinity for a dining room or a kitchen. He is usually looked upon as domestic, because he unconsciously clings to the home, where the food is kept.
>
> He saves things. In fact, his wife complains about the way he keeps the home and the back yard cluttered up with junk. He is a conservative. (Calvin Coolidge and John D. Rockefeller were of this sign.) He may hide money away in strange places. The women may be babyish (and so are the men), welcoming protection, and usually drawing it to themselves. Such people are always interested in shortages, and will buy up a short supply, in order to resell it at a profit. These people are great traders, and are constantly testing you

to see how ripe you may be for a trade that would be profitable to them. The men have a favorite expression, and no matter how much they accumulate, they will keep repeating it. It goes, 'I'm just a poor boy trying to get along.' This expression always seems to be a dead giveaway. It will peg them every time. The factor of arrogant pride is completely lacking. They are humble and not above begging. They make excellent salesmen, because they sense what the client needs, or they will study carefully until they learn...

There is never complete relaxation, for something might go wrong, and there is ever a fear of poverty in old age. Such fears are ever being fed... Yet, these people are kind. When John D. Rockefeller became the wealthiest man in America, he became noted for giving away newly coined dimes. They cost no more than old worn out dimes. The primitive still operates.

A study of the birth dates of 500 men listed in WHO'S WHO IN COMMERCE AND INDUSTRY by the writer (Later published in SEASON OF BIRTH by Dr. Ellsworth Huntington of Yale University.), revealed that Cancer men are the most successful in the accumulation of money."[1]

Years ago I had a client who had a Cancerian mother. The mother had survived WW II in France and suffered greatly as a teenager. The client and her brothers were always hungry as children and underfed by their Cancerian mother. Yet, she would take them down to the basement to show them all the canned food she had stored in the pantry! She just had to know that she would never starve again, even at the expense of her own children. This is an extreme example but the mother had grown up in extreme circumstances. She had not dealt with her compulsive need to be surrounded with food. This could have just as well had been money in the bank since it is easily converted into food. In hard times, Cancerians can be the saviors of the day by coming up with the necessary funds to avoid an even greater loss.

The next most primitive and fundamental drive or emotion is the sex drive, the SURVIVAL of the Family. Can the spouse and children be protected to perpetuate the bloodline? Can the spouse be kept safe within the family orb so that only one's genes are passed onto the next generation? How can the spouse be kept faithful? This is the fundamental drive of Scorpio as Fixed Water, ruled by Mars and associated with the sex organs. There are three symbols for this sign, the scorpion, the snake and the eagle. The first two are about the lower compulsive side of the sex drive that manifests as jealousy, possessiveness and excessive controlling behavior. If the sex drive is not understood or worse controlled, it can become like a dark monster that lurks in the deep and dark that is impulsive or can rage. Religion generally stifles this basic impulse to the point of warping its expression with rules and 'thou shall not's.' This has been especially true for women when society characterizes them as virgins or whores for expressing their sexual desires. The eagle is such a contrast to the scorpion but it is the high expression of the sex drive to have executive ability, to protect the family or corporation from the rest of the world. This is the need to keep 'personal' information in the 'family.' The family or family business is to be protected at all costs from the public.

Carl Payne Tobey writes:

"This is the next most primitive of all life purposes. The life of the family began before that of the individual and extends beyond the life of the individual. Are you going to continue the family? Will someone steal your mate? By making sex a desired act, nature endeavors to perpetuate the family. The ancients associated Scorpio with the sex organs, but because of the quick temper that is also associated with Scorpio, there may be an additional connection with the adrenal glands...

At birth, this dynamic is always conditioned. There is almost an infinite variety of possible patterns sex life can follow, and some of them can be very destructive. There are stimulants, curbs and shock absorbers. The sex dynamic is powerful and not something that can be handled successfully by invoking one set of rules for all persons, which can be a dangerous procedure on the part of society. When insanity involves violence, it also involves the sex dynamic. All other violence involves the sex dynamic directly or indirectly.

Pains and fevers also have an association with this dynamic, but this will not include all types of pain. It will not include a toothache. We discuss this elsewhere. As we have stated, pain rises as the result of unconscious interpretation, it can be closely identified with sex. The sadist has to inflict pain to become sexually aroused, while the masochist has to endure pain to become so aroused.[an afflicted Mars]

It is an odd circumstance worthy of investigation by the medical profession that the astrological and mathematical factors that create excessive sex desires under some circumstances will be accompanied by biological conditions necessitating surgery under other circumstances. This suggests the possibility that many physical ailments are unhealthy functioning of the sexual system...

This dynamic can express itself in temper and violence, when the unconscious interpretive apparatus interprets an incident as a threat to family survival, but the force can be poorly directed. It misses its mark...

If the boss gives Mr. Smith a bad day, Mr. Smith may go home and beat up his wife or children. He does not beat up the boss. The force follows the course of least resistance. Children are often the objective because they can't defend themselves. The release of emotion follows that course of least resistance. If the boss himself has this dynamic stimulated, everyone at the office may have a bad day. If the teacher has her family survival dynamic touched off the night before, the children must be punished. The husband may love his wife and hate a man who admires her, so he beats up his wife. Children are probably the chief victims of the misdirection of this dynamic.

Although vindictiveness is associated with Scorpio, there is an unconscious primitive cunning for this dynamic fails to function before superior power. It seldom directs its force against a more powerful opponent, but will submit to and endure pain on such occasions, and this is where masochist tendencies appear to begin. In sadism, the desire to inflict pain is aimed toward the loved one instead of a possible competitor. Jealousy arouses the sex passion. This dynamic can express itself in love or hatred. Love brings family continuation. Hatred is intended to protect the family. If the mate is indiscreet in sexual relations, love may be translated into hatred. The dynamic causes compulsions. When dominated by it, individuals do not understand nor control their own behavior. They are automatons. A harmless incident may be followed by rage due to faulty functioning on the part of the unconscious interpretive apparatus. It may be much as if a demon has taken over. The individual may be conscious of what he is doing without having control. Possible consequences are hidden from him. He is blind to them. When the rage is over, there may be sorrow, remorse and the most apologetic reaction...

Conflicts involving this dynamic are perhaps the most vital studied in astrology. They involve pain, violence, murder, rape, and matters that occupy much space in sensational magazines and newspapers...Accidents are usually caused by faulty functioning of this dynamic. One's attention is usually placed elsewhere, often in another moment of time.

This dynamic can express itself in temper and violence, when the unconscious interpretive apparatus interprets an incident as a threat to family survival, but the force can be poorly directed. It misses its mark... [Scorpio is] characteristic of the surgeon, for all surgery seems linked with this dynamic. He cannot do his work efficiently if he faints at the sight of blood.

Scorpio supplies ability to direct others and obey commands of superiors, often producing good military men. Theodore Roosevelt and General George Patton are to be included. There is the ability to arouse emotion in others, as demonstrated by the two outstanding evangelists of this century, Billy Sunday and Billy Graham. These men were driven by the sex dynamic."[2]

I once had a married friend that had a heavy dose of Scorpio and Cancer in her chart. She had an open marriage with her spouse so that they could have other sex partners. She talked baby talk to her spouse and waxed off her pubic hair to seem more baby-like sexually to her spouse.

The third basic emotional drive is to be a member of a social/ cultural group. Humans are social animals that live within a culture. We want to be members of our social group. This is the need to belong to more than just one's family but to a social group. This is seen with the beat of drums that drive a group into the unison of trance or dance whether that is primitive, hip-hop, rap or a rave with trance dance music. It is the need to support the social group, to have common values or a common purpose, to melt into the group mind of music or dance. Pisces is the sign that is the need to belong; it is the survival of the weak, the opposite of Darwin's survival of the fittest. This sign creates the need to support the weaker elements of our society, to promote the non-conformists, to support the artists or shamans of our group. Pisces is Mutable Water and is strongly associated with the feet and ruled by Neptune (it's old ruler was Jupiter). This is the source of psychic ability, the sympathy for small animals, the group mind that drives individuals to act beyond their personal norms to act like a mob or riot. It is the religious experience of mediation for nirvana or taking LSD to be one with creation. The Pisces person can feel so deeply that there can be an addictive need for drugs or alcohol. And on the other side, Pisces is the dreamer, the idealist. This is the creative person that produces fantasy on stage or in a movie. They have the ability to take a group of people on an emotional ride of drama or science fiction, to suspend harsh reality for a period of time.

Pisces points to a very ancient part of our biology, like the reptilian brain that can go on autopilot, taking us to places in our dreams and imagination that is unconscious and subterranean. There is a primitive instinct that a Piscean may follow that is beyond social laws which is why so many Neptunian people can be associated with criminals, the mentally ill or social outcasts. There is an inner knowledge that cannot be verbalized. An instinct that is followed with the gut, a body intuition that is felt, not thought out. This is the sign of the poet or the homeless drug addict. They could be a superstar of music or movies because they can speak to the cultural group in a way that resonates. Please view this Ted Talk by Dr. Frans de Waal about this principle just being discovered by scientists[3]

Tobey states:

"The third is the strangest, most mysterious and perhaps most interesting, of all survival dynamics. It is a principle overlooked by Darwin, for it involves survival of the weak.

The interests of the individual and the family may be ignored. Socialism is merely an expression of this dynamic. We also see its better manifestation in such organizations as The Society for the Prevention

of Cruelty to Animals, the Society for the Prevention
of Cruelty to Children, The Salvation Army, The Red
Cross. We see it in the erection of hospitals and other
similar institutions. We see it in social legislation. The
fight for equal rights for the Negro came with Neptune,
ruler of Pisces, in Scorpio.

Unfortunately, the negative manifestations are more
often in evidence, because Man is having difficulty
in discovering his relationship with society and his
families' relations with society. Maladjustment in
the functioning of this dynamic leads to insanity and
illnesses of other forms. There is utter confusion.
'Primitive' astrological interpretations linked Pisces
with prisons, hospitals, institutions, the underworld,
scandal, fraud, deception, crime, secretiveness, alcohol,
drugs, and anesthetics. When we see how the pieces fit
together, they look less primitive.

Sympathy and compassion are qualities of Pisces.
They are greater than any respect for law, order
or convention. These become secondary. The law
is circumvented. The objective must be achieved,
secretly if necessary, but very often an illegal course is
followed. The effort to pack the US Supreme Court was
a manifestation of this dynamic. Socialism need not be
considered as a product of Man. It is the functioning
of the social survival dynamic. There is compassion
for the underdog, the downtrodden, the abnormal, the
sick, the weak, the beggar, the criminal, the servants,
the employees, the lower classes, lower beings, pets,
animals, the alcoholic, the dope addict, etc... A woman
client who had inherited a good deal of money and had
no cause for any fear of insecurity was considerably
mixed up. Surgery had been employed to remove her
gall bladder and appendix, which had grown faulty,
but she continued confused. Her birth chart showed a
terrific conflict between the second and third survival
dynamics [Mars and Neptune], a conflict between
social survival and family survival.

She confessed that throughout her marital life she had
committed continuous adultery with numerous men,
and that her four children were of different fathers.

She covered her indiscretions well. She was suspected by neither her husband nor society, for she was a leader in various philanthropic organizations and highly regarded in her community. Her indiscretions always involved men from a lower social strata, often men she employed.

We begin to see the light when she tells us that her behavior was not so much the result of any sex passion as the result of a deep feeling within her own emotions than men needed her. It gave her satisfaction to believe that she was filling a social need. Unconsciously, she was helping men continue the existence of families. It was sort of a communist family institution. She had the money to support the children."[4]

Since 2012 Neptune has entered its own sign of Pisces and will be there until 2025. The fight for marriage equality by homosexuals had been fiercely resisted but since Neptune left Capricorn (the sign of legal resistance and maintenance of the status quo) the USA and many other countries have allowed same sex marriage. The USA federal government made marijuana illegal in the 1930's and suddenly after many years of the War on Drugs, half of the 50 states have partially legalized it. Most of this acceptance of pot by society has come with Neptune in Pisces. Colorado and Washington have fully legalized marijuana in 2012 and 23 states have recognized medical marijuana. More will occur and either the federal government will legalize pot or just ignore the old law that is becoming out of fashion. Many states and federal authorities have been releasing convicted drug criminals with early release. There has been a change of attitude about the incarceration of drug related crimes.

It is the function of the Earth signs to give order, constraint and form to the three Water signs of emotion. It is a geometric balance that each Water sign is opposed by it's restraining Earth sign.

Cancer	Individual survival opposed by	Capricorn
Scorpio	Family survival opposed by	Taurus
Pisces	Group survival opposed by	Virgo

The Earth signs give self-control but if there is too much Earth, it can lead to frustration and the inability to react in a timely manner. There is a general resistance to change or an overt expression of feelings if the Earth signs are dominant in the natal horoscope. Duty, responsibility and tradition are all Earth sign moderators to contain the overflow or flooding of feelings that can get out of control.

Capricorn is a Cardinal Earth sign that restricts the excessive greed and need of Cancer that can never have enough. It is ruled by Saturn and is associated with the bones, joints and teeth. Capricorn is strongly associated with laws that restrict behaviors. About 80% of most state laws are about property rights. Robbery is deemed illegal unless it is the Bankers that are doing the stealing. The laws are written to protect the Banks from loss. In 2005 US bankruptcy laws were rewritten so student loans could never be forgiven, the Bankers will collect it from your pension or social security until death! Capricornians tend to conform to the rules their parents and teachers give them early in life. There is a need for accomplishment and recognition by their superiors or elders. They can study and achieve advanced degrees because of their ability for self-control. But too much duty can lead to depression or becoming dull with too much responsibility and routine. Overwork can lead to illness and fatigue. With balance, Capricorns can let go and give themselves more freedom but they need to maintain their public image. If they break social standards, it will be out of town, somewhere they are not known. The challenge comes later in life when beliefs and standards that served them well in youth are now out of synch with current social standards. Then Capricorn can become unwanted baggage, the scapegoat; they can get locked into the past. Just as joints and bones can become frozen and arthritic, Capricorn can become fossilized in the past. Much like old laws that are never removed but remain for persecution upon occasion.

Tobey states:

> "When a person is born strongly under Capricorn, it is the tendency to give in to one's oppressors, to conform, to adjust one's self to the environment, to be a good boy, to save and be thrifty, to accept authority, to curb one's appetites and keep them under control, to do the unpleasant things in life because they have to be done, to place great value on material quantities, to do things the hard way, to assume great responsibility, to be the goat, possibly to rise to high places only to wear one's self out and succumb, to turn away from anything that promises quick and easy profits on the grounds that any such promises are unsound and the profits highly improbable, to be pessimistic and depressive, to always see the negative possibilities and try to insure

against them without being able to see more favorable possibilities, to take a dark view of the future, to be sound and practical and to judge the future by the past.

In a great many cases, we find the person, in whose birth chart this Capricorn REACTOR is strong, very successful in early life. He meets with approval of older people whenever he goes. His reliability is of value. His responsibility is something that is noted. He is pushed forward by older men, because they can depend on him. He develops good contacts, but there comes a day when these older men begin to die off. More and more of them die off. Ultimately, Capricorn is surrounded by younger men. He continues to live according to the rules of the old masters. The younger men are without respect for these old masters and are unimpressed. His views are considered as obsolete and reactionary. He is no longer appreciated, but instead, is regarded as an obstacle. Others feel that his usefulness has been served. He doesn't fit into the new order of things. He can't understand it. 'After all, the world got along for a long time without these new-fangled ideas. These young men are apt to wreck the world. They are unsound. ' He feels that they lack experience. If old Mr. Goat were still alive, he would see them, but Mr. Goat died some time back and can't influence things now.

CAPRICORN no longer fits into the picture. The world's evaluation of him has been deflated. He is a sad man. He is very depressed. There is no longer a place in the world for him. Statistics have shown that the manic depressive is born strongly under this Capricorn REACTOR."[5]

For the family to flourish, it needs a home, an environment to house and protect the family. This is the main purpose of Taurus as Fixed Earth, ruled by Venus* and associated with the neck and voice. Real estate, land and property associated with one's home is Taurean. This sign represents the past heredity from one's parents and grandparents. It is the physical defense to house and protect the family. It is also a limiter to the sex drive. As it's opposite, Scorpio can be easy to anger, but Taurus is difficult to move, it can be sluggish and have delayed reactions. Taureans are noted for a slow burn but when egged on, the defense of family can be immense and prolonged. A battle can lead to annihilation of the enemy.

Tobey said:

"Taurus likes big homes, lots of land. It is all part of
an unconscious building of a fort to protect the family.
Taurus likes to do everything in a big way. Whether he
is prosperous or not, he is apt to look prosperous. He
is a builder. His original inclination to build a fort may
take other forms. He might be a contractor. He makes
a good engineer. He understands weight, volume and
density. He likes to be big himself. He thinks in terms
of quantity. He likes things when they are big. This all
stems from the original purpose of building a big fort
to protect the family. Taurus is FIXED EARTH. The
bigger the fort, the greater the family security and the
greater the opportunity for family survival.

Although TAURUS may take on the family virtues, it
is just as easy to take on the family faults. There is an
unconscious urge to imitate the parents or grandparents,
to acquire their habits, to continue their traditions.
There may be too much consideration for what the family
may think. There may be a lack of initiative, because
it is more comfortable at home with the family, where
one can sleep. There seems to be a voice that constantly
says, 'Don't do what the family would not want you to do.'
When asked why he never married, an elderly bachelor
told us, 'I thought a great deal of my family. I never felt
that I could marry any girl who would meet the approval
of the family, and I knew well that my family could never
approve of the kind of a girl I would want to marry.'

There can be inability to get away from the old part of
the family, and go forth to produce the new family in a
new home. Such ties are not easily broken. They can be
carried to extremes. It may be difficult to accept new
ideas. The old family ideas have long, deep roots. Taurus
wants to be proud of his heredity. He is likely to know
as much as possible about his genealogy. Stubbornness
is a characteristic. Taurus may be sluggish and slow to
grasp things. It may take much education before he can
grasp the abstract side of things. He is coming out of a
fog. He becomes a prisoner of dogma. Yet, he can be the
worst enemy of dogma, because he will fight dogma with
dogma."[6]

Taureans are the land barons of the zodiac. If they can afford a ranch, they will buy land and build. If not, then a view of a wide expanse will do. They can become very settled in their home, preferring not to leave it. Once the furniture is placed, it stays there. Comfort is the keyword, they build a nest and enjoy it.

The third Earth sign of Virgo is the counterbalance to Pisces. It is Mutable Earth, ruled by Mercury and is associated with the intestines. This a practical sign that is given to details and minutia. Pisces is nebulous while Virgos want to get the rules right. They know what is socially acceptable. It is strongly associated with the fashion industry. Fashion is about conforming to current dressing trends and being part of the in-crowd. Virgos note the details of proper manners whether it's in a boardroom or in a rock concert, they will dress and act appropriately. This sign is associated with the intestines and the mottos of 'you are what you eat'. Diet and food choices are made consciously and very likely vitamins are used. They can be the health nuts regarding food trends. The phase "he didn't have the guts" refers to Virgos ability to work long and hard, to put their nose to the grindstone to finish a job. Not surprisingly, this sign's weak point can be in the intestines with too much stress expressed with worry and chronic digestive problems like inflammatory bowel problems. I once had a supervisor that dressed very properly for business meetings and on weekends put on a complete Hell's Angels outfit to go motorcycling on his Harley. The contrast was breathtaking.

Tobey said:

"Nature appears to have understood that if you give everything to the weak, the result is disintegration. Sympathizing with the weak and suffering with them is not a cure, and so nature provided a REACTOR to containing these emotional qualities.

A man is too weak to survive. First, we try to cure him. We give him medical or other attention, and then we try to find a job for him...

Astrology has associated VIRGO with the working classes, the laborers, labor unions, also with diets, medicine and attempts to heal.
As in the case of all EARTH signs, VIRGO strives to be practical. If you have a sick man, make him well. Make him useful. Find him a job. Get him functioning, make use of his physical anatomy. Turn him into a productive

factor... That is being practical.

VIRGO people as a whole are workers, often to the point of frustration. They are efficient. Being close observers, they don't miss any details. They do a good job. They make the most valuable employee. There is a great power of concentration, which is the opposite characteristic found in connection with the Social Survival Dynamic itself (Pisces). Pisces is a dreamer, misses the details, but observes the broader pattern of the whole.

Somebody has to do the work, and VIRGO is there, waiting to carry on. 'All work and no play makes Jack a dull boy.'

It is the inclination of Virgo to over-work, to exclude all else. The work to be done assumes too great a significance." [7]

In contrast, Pisces will emotionally bleed for the weak, and the sick. They may prefer to socialize with the non-conformist. Virgo will build and staff a hospital for the sick, built and staff a prison for the criminal and try to reform the non-conformist. Virgo will support the weak by trying to make them stronger. Pisces just feels for them.

There are many astrology books that give great detail on each sign but rarely do they explain the deeper emotional drives that these signs manifest. If the basic psychological underpinnings are understood, then behaviors can be understood. These are the fundamental motivations behind actions and behaviors. Half of the zodiac is represented as feminine but it is more accurately represented in terms of time. In the ancient world the archetype of feminine was a global representation of the duality of past vs. future, passive vs. active, etc. Half of the zodiac represents the Past. These are old, deep, primitive, instinctual behaviors that are generally unconscious. They are formed in childhood but some part of this is hereditary that is imprinted into our genes. It is a strange dynamic between astrology and heredity as the first seems to point to or activate our gene patterns into forward expression versus recessive genes or heredity that is never expressed but may carry forward to another generation. This is the great dilemma in our times. Where does the astrological expression leave off and the social developmental behavior start? Where does free will begin and fated karmic expression stop? It does appear that 'know thy self' with conscious insight helps to curb and modify the unconscious instincts. It can free the individual from automatic behaviors but it takes an active effort. Most psychologists help individuals to reveal themselves so that other choices can be made. Carl Jung called it self-actualization. He believed in bringing the dark underside of emotions into the light of examination. Jung's goal was to integrate the dark part of us with the conscious part of ourselves. He believed that the scary monster (Jung's Shadow) inside an individual was a source of great personal power that could be harnessed. Astrology is a great aid in the examination of self. It is like a road map to understanding ourselves and to understand the dynamics of what a particular time means, how long it will last and what is the purpose that is pushing us.

Footnotes

1. Tobey, Carl Payne, Correspondence Course Lesson 2, 1957.
2. Ibid.
3. http://www.ted.com/talks/frans_de_waal_do_animals_have_ morals?language=en
4. Tobey, Correspondence Course.
5. Ibid.
6. Ibid.
7. Tobey, Lesson 3.

*Venus is the co-ruler of Libra and Taurus. In the future it is likely that two planets outside the orbit of Pluto will become the rulers of Gemini and Taurus. In 2005, Eris was discovered as a planetoid outside the orbit of Pluto and almost its size. It is a likely candidate for rulership of Taurus. This could be the historic planet Y and there is a remaining planet Z to be assigned to Gemini.

Fire and Air
Signs of the Future

The prior chapter dealt with the six past signs of the zodiac and now the other half are about the Future. The ancient term was Masculine but as astrology deals with time, referring to them as Future signs is more appropriate. Imprinting happens at birth but behavior dynamics occur throughout our lifetime. Are we pulled to express our heredity or to create something new? A horoscope is always a balancing of Now with the Past and Future, whether it is for someone's birth or an event. What is the nature or quality of that time? Is the past of heredity, habits, convention or routines dominating or is this a moment in time calling for a new definition, a different creation or new expression? Usually it's a mixture of both since the zodiac is evenly divided between past and future but if there is a dominance of planets in past signs, the theme will be to keep conventions in place. If the planets are dominated in future signs, then the emergence of something new is more likely. It can never be all past or all future since the planets are by definition balanced between past and future themselves. This is the push-pull between keeping what has been and pushing for what will be.

Fire in the ancient times was the archetype of energy, drive or ambition to create something new. In astrology, there were three types of Fire.

Individual Non-Survival	Leo	Future
Family Non-Survival	Aries	Future
Social Non-Survival	Sagittarius	Future

Leo is a Fixed Fire sign ruled by the Sun and associated with the heart. The Sun is the energy of self-expression and the Sun in any of the twelve zodiac signs takes on the characteristics of each sign. Leos want self-expression to carve a new path or direction for themselves. They love attention and to draw a following of people into their sphere of influence. This is the sign of the showman, king or leader. They can be magnificent, dramatic and charismatic. They have the desire to become more, to push themselves into a new direction or expression. There is an energetic restlessness to expand their influence. Leos don't wait for opportunities, they create them. Tobey said:

> "Ancient astrologers portrayed Leo as the Lion, the king of all the beasts, and the symbols of the zodiac were sometimes referred to as the beasts. Leo was associated and identified with the heart, and when we have serious afflictions to the Individual Non-Survival Dynamic, we often find them accompanied by heart attacks. We might say that a heart attack is the result of an unconscious or superconscious desire not to survive in the present form. The writer has often noted that, prior to a heart attack, the individual was irritable, fed up with the status quo, and desirous of some kind of change that seemed out of the question to him. Life in its then-present form was intolerable to him. It has been noted that, while some people make broad changes under some astrological circumstances, others die of heart attacks under the same circumstances. In one such case, a man was all set to make a very broad change and move his family to another part of the country, without knowing how either he or the family were to survive in the new land. Close associates prevailed upon him to change his mind. Two days later, he died of a heart attack."[1]

The prior chapter discussed that the past heredity of the family was with Scorpio and Taurus. Those two signs represent what has already been, the perpetuation of the family through the sex drive and protecting the family. But what of the children that are to come? Aries is Cardinal Fire, ruled by Pluto and associated with the head. It is associated with a burning desire to strike out in new directions, to be a pioneer, to be commander of their own ship. This sign must be the boss; they are headstrong and know what they want. Aries has the will, vision and energy to create its own future. Many times Aries types have many conflicts with family authority, so they strike out on their own. They emotionally don't need their family of origin, they want to create their own, either in business or unconsciously with the children they will create. They would rather be 'a big fish in a little pond than a little fish in a big pond.' Aries wants to create their own empire. They can be attracted to others from a different race, country or background. Unconsciously they are attempting to bring in new hereditary genes to create their future children. Or in business, they have the need to create their own vision of a business that they can command and direct. Tobey said:

> "Study the difference between Aries and Scorpio. The
> latter sign impulsively fights for the interests of the
> family. You hurt a Scorpio if you attack any part of his
> family, but Aries is more apt to think of the family as part
> of him, and if the family is not part of him, something
> happens. There may be a break. When a large number
> of Aries people are studied, it is remarkable how many
> cases we find where there is an unexplainable break
> with some member of the family. It may be a parent,
> a brother, a sister or a child, but Aries has a definite
> conception of what the future of the family is to be, and
> if any member of the family proves to be an obstruction
> to that plan, there is a break. It may be subtle. It may
> not show too strongly on the surface. The Aries child
> may slip away from the family, take up with others,
> pioneer, and go his way.
>
> The Aries individual may move to a distant place. There
> is no apparent discord. He may keep in touch with the
> family and be on distant good terms with its members.
> He will do anything to help them, send them money,
> but he has his own life to live. Unconsciously, he is out
> to change the hereditary strain. He may marry one of
> foreign birth or someone quite far removed from his
> own heredity. There is the superconscious urge to create
> a new strain. He may accept, into the family, persons of
> different blood. An adopted child may be just as dear
> to him as his own. He is out to create his own empire.
> In this new empire, his word is law. So long as everyone
> conforms, it will be a peaceful existence, but if you have
> different ideas, they are not acceptable. They will be
> kindly vetoed.
>
> The soul of the dictator is found in Aries, but only
> within his own domain. His children are supposed to
> obey. He lives their lives. He knows what is best for
> them, and he will map their careers. They are supposed
> to follow his course."[2]

The third Fire sign is Sagittarius, which is Mutable Fire, ruled
by Jupiter and associated with the thighs and liver. Sagittarius cares
about making its social group or culture better than it currently

is. They see a need to change mores, values, government, religion or education for the better. They have a sense of how their society could benefit with a vision of a better future. They are natural reformers. They use education to expand the vision of others, to enroll others into their vision of what social change can mean to all. To expand their vision for a better world, they may become religious ministers, politicians or any advocate for change to benefit society or a group. They voice their opinions and at times can put 'their foot into their mouth' by ignoring social politeness and not being more diplomatic. They have intuition or an ability to sense the right direction to take for discoveries. There is a natural instinct to merge separate or distinct concepts together into a unified whole, to see the 'big picture.' Tobey said:

> "It is ever the purpose of Sagittarius to change and alter the form and ideas of society, and the chief way in which this dynamic manifests is through education, science, travel, religion and reform... Sagittarians are noted for their outspokenness and ability to shoot straight to the mark. It is hard for them to hold something back. What they think is so, they have to state. This is a natural tendency to teach what they consider their own wisdom.
>
> They may both seek truth, but the wisdom of Pisces always stems from the past, while the wisdom of Sagittarius stems from the future. Pisces attempts to preserve the wisdom of the past, and is more representative of mysticism, cults, churches, the occult, esotericism, theosophy, reincarnation, Karma, spiritualism, etc.
>
> Sagittarius represents more what we would call the creative scientist. He has 'flashes'. With a million possibilities to choose from, he occasionally picks out the right one. He has a hunch. He tests it, and it works. The inventor, at least to himself, recognizes these hunches. Most scientific discoveries had their inception when somebody followed a hunch...
>
> His purpose is not just to reform himself. Leo reforms himself. Aries reforms the family, but Sagittarius wants to reform society. It is not enough of him to accept a truth. He wants to teach it. He could go on alone, but

this doesn't appear to give satisfaction...

An inspection of the birth dates of German spies caught in this country during World War II showed that more than half of them were born with the Sun in Sagittarius. They were caught merely because they were too free in expressing their views. Pisces would have been more secretive... Sagittarius is not noted for diplomacy. While Pisces avoids persecution by being subtle and secretive, Sagittarius asks for it by shouting his views from the housetops. It would seem that the Pisces 'soul' knows about the persecutions of history. He instinctively knows that you can be persecuted for telling the truth."[3]

There is always a balance of energies in astrology. The force of the Fire signs are to push, drive and create the future but like the Water signs, there needs to be another factor to direct the energy. The Air signs stand for the intelligence needed to take raw energy and give it form and direction. Air might have meant the ethereal to most ancient cultures. Air represented the 'ideal' as an abstraction of form was a concept of the ancient world. It was a manifestation of God, the Creator, or of Nature. They did not have the modern concept of 'intelligence' but they were aware there was an abstract world of ideas that existed prior to form becoming manifest reality. Today we just say 'intelligence' represent ideas as omnipresent and the creative mind can discern glimpses of this world of ideas. To balance the energy of Fire, the three intelligence signs are:

Individual Non-Survival Guide	Aquarius	Future
Family Non-Survival Guide	Libra	Future
Social Non-Survival Guide	Gemini	Future

Aquarius is Fixed Air, ruled by Uranus (formerly Saturn) and associated with the ankles, the nervous system and with blood. This is an outgoing sign, just as Leo is the extrovert, Aquarius is too. Aquarius can live their lives 20 years or more ahead of their time. They tend to have innovative ideas that are too far out for their peers or elders. It generally takes the next generation to 'get' them. Tobey said:

"The Aquarian is an abstractionist who sees things, not as they were, not as they are, but as they will be.

He unconsciously senses the trend ahead. The process of unconscious calculation is ever going on. Instead of identifying security with the past, he sees only the imperfections of the past, taking the good for granted. The past and present stimulate only restlessness and irritability. He never figures that it can't happen here. Instead, he is sure that it will, and he is alert for it. He is inclined to view material things as responsibilities rather than as assets. If they hold him down or limit him, he wants to break away from them. He harbors the spirit of the hobo. He likes to keep on going on. Because he always sees how things could be done, he is inventive. Evangeline Adams wrote that these people tend to live a hundred years ahead of their times. They often accomplish the impossible... They were not hampered by insecurity. They were not trying to perpetuate the past. They were non-conformists. They were never willing to leave well enough alone. They were not content to live and let live. Their purpose could hardly be called survival. They fear not what is ahead. They do not fear death, nor are they worried about starvation. Ties are easily broken. Time is changed, and they want change. They think in terms of motion, not in terms of stationary objects. They love action and excitement. There is a sadistic delight in seeing the old order of things destroyed. Ideas are more important than money... Unlike Cancer or Capricorn, Aquarius is not conservative. He is radical. All men who turn up with a new and better idea are looked upon as radicals in their time. They are not considered as intelligent, but are looked upon as 'crackpots'...

When [Uranus] is afflicted, the result is terrific impatience and irritability with the present form, and the individual is called destructive. A boy may have a yen for throwing rocks through plate glass windows. There can be sarcasm and a critical attitude toward everything anyone else may do. To destroy is a thrill. We often see a person destroy himself by means of an 'accident'. Unconsciously, he wants to get on with things, which he cannot do in his present form. When studying accidents or illness astrologically, it is always well to look carefully to see what purpose has been served by the accident or illness. You will find that a very definite unconscious purpose has been served."[4]

The spotlight is fine with Aquarius, they like the attention but if they consider others to be stupid, they can have a biting sense of humor to the point of cruelty and they love the element of surprise, to shock others. In their youth, they are likely to be considered, odd, unconventional, weird or incomprehensible by the older generation. They simply live ahead of their time. It is likely that public recognition comes thirty or more years later when a new generation of people is grown up who can appreciate their ideas and actions. Or it can be long after death that genius is recognized. Aquarius embraces change, they like a change of people, environment or work. It's a chance to do something new and exciting.

Libra is the balancing sign to Aries. It is Cardinal Air, ruled by Venus and is associated with the kidneys. Its symbol is the scales, the balancing of two sides equally, like an algebraic equation. Libra is strongly associated with mathematics, classical music and architecture because all three subjects require the balancing of elements to create a harmonic effect in a building or musical composition. Librans can be the diplomats of the world; they can argue both sides of a debate, see both sides and try to harmonize with their enemies or opponents. They have the strength to hold to their own principles but there is no need for an argument. Venus and Libra is the power of attraction. It can draw people together. Unconsciously, it is attracting new heredity into the Family. An important new lover or spouse is recognized across a room full of people. It is the power of attraction that draws people together whether as friends or lovers. It is the recognition of 'the other.' Someone else that is a reflection of what we like. It is associated with fraternities, sororities or any social organization. Social organizations have a common purpose to draw like-minded people together. But its deepest purpose is to attract others for the creation of a new kind of family or children. Tobey said:

> "It is quite possible that the scales represented the principle of balance in nature. The beautiful requires balance. We find beauty and balance in nature. We find beauty and balance throughout the study of mathematics and physics. We find this GUIDE prominent in the horoscopes of the best mathematicians and physicists, and the greatest mathematicians have always been men who saw beauty in mathematics. The beautiful woman is one whose features and form are perfectly balanced...is to make the family more beautiful, to give

it better balance, symmetry and design in its form. This Guide attracts to beauty. It endeavors to improve the family-to-be by attracting to a mate who is more perfectly designed mathematically, a beautiful girl or a handsome man. The most beautiful woman is often born when Libra is on the eastern horizon.

When a man or woman is drawn to a beautiful or handsome mate, there is unconscious improvement in the form and appearance of children-to-be. It is a form of BALANCE when the male and female seek each other. The magnet attracts the needle. The earth attracts the Moon and the Moon attracts the earth...

The type of people we seek as friends is determined by [Venus]... When a young person begins to seek mixed company in a social way, this GUIDE is directing things. The young person becomes less tied to his parents. The breaking away process is beginning to develop. This is not a sex factor which is separate [Mars and Scorpio]... He begins to prefer the associations of the pretty girl to that of his family. This is new and refreshing, but two families want to survive, and half a loaf is better than none. Each family can survive on a 50% ratio. Ultimately, [Mars]... operates, and there is sex. A child is born. It is 50% of each family. Two families have survived to a lesser ratio. The Family Non-Survival Dynamic and its GUIDE continually operate to prevent the possibility of incest. A brother-sister relationship would give 100% survival to the heredity strain. There would be but two parents and two grandparents. Nothing new would have been added... Most Libra people underestimate their own potentials. They are not keenly interested in achieving fame. Sometimes they find it embarrassing and as a rule they would prefer the society of smaller groups of their own choosing."[5]

Gemini is the opposing sign to Sagittarius. It is Mutable Air, ruled by Mercury (but a likely new ruler could be beyond Eris) and associated with the lungs and arms. It is always seen in duality in its sign of the twins since more twins are born under this sign. This is changing with artificial insemination and planned deliveries so the old pattern is changing. Duality is a strong theme for this sign because Geminis can hold many ideas and concepts in their minds at one time. This is the sign of the writer, comic and commentator of society. They can find the humor in a situation or injustice and make fun of an event or person. Humor is used for social change. Gemini has the bright ideas to make their social group better for the future so they use humor to let the bitter pills go down easier. They can be glib and talkative, wanting to communicate their ideas to others. But the deeper point is to direct or guide their group or culture to a better future. Many times the ideas flow so fast; the words cannot keep up with their minds. They can bounce between people and social groups looking for change and stimulus. A change of scenery, a need to move around, short projects are best for their restless minds. They can be a jack-of-all-trades, master of none since their interest can wane if it takes too much time. They are quick at grasping a subject and learning new skills, it just comes easy for them. Sticking with it is another matter. Chaos can rein in their environment, tidying up or organizing just isn't interesting or necessary to them. Tobey said:

> "Gemini is always shifting around from one thing to another. It is a truly intellectual sign, but an army is needed to complete all the things that Gemini starts... Mechanical ability is quite common to this sign, because these people grasp and understand abstract mechanical principles. A Gemini woman can probably change a tire or fix her own car if she has to... These people make good editors. They never bore people because they always have some new angle on something. Their interest of tomorrow is different from that of yesterday. To some people, they may seem inconsistent. The sign represents mental change and that goes on forever. Gemini people like to travel mentally and physically. A constant change of environment usually suits them fine. There can be a good deal of nervousness, restlessness and impatience. They want to get on to tomorrow."[6]

The point of these descriptions is not to go over every characteristic and feature of each sign but to understand the driving motivation and principle represented by each sign. These twelve signs are archetypes that have far deeper meanings and expressions that the people and events that surround us. There are very long time periods and patterns in planetary movements that take many generations to repeat and there are shorter repetitive patterns like the inner planets. It is easy to see an entire cycle of Saturn in 29 years, Jupiter in 12 years, or Mars in two years. But the patterns of

Uranus, Neptune and Pluto are beyond one lifetime. This creates unique time periods of events and people that are similar to the past but never identical. It's valuable to study past events and people to understand these twelve principles of expression, especially when three new ruling planets have been discovered (Uranus, Neptune and Pluto). There are new patterns to analysis. The probability that two more additional planetary rulers are to be assigned to Taurus and Gemini will only add to the discovery of new patterns, yet the principles of Taurus and Gemini are already present. Their nature can be analyzed to then look for these future rulers that have those same characteristics.

Understanding these twelve foundational principles provides a guide for astrologers to deepen their understanding as they face events in their own lives and those around them to make new observations of these archetypes. Seeing world events unfold around us with astrological insight gives a deeper understanding of the dynamics behind actions taken by world leaders. There are global events that follow astrological principles that are being expressed constantly, if we only have the eyes to witness the patterns. Tobey said:

> "Just as any mathematical problem has to have an answer containing certain characteristics, there is often but one way in which the future can happen, for the future also has to have certain characteristics, and astrology will ALWAYS tell us the characteristics of the future. Although the astrologer may err in his details of the future, there is never a reason why he should err in his calculations of the characteristics of the future. These are always plainly written.[7]

The nature of the archetypes is more important than each detailed characteristic description because once the principle is learned, then its many expressions can be recognized. These twelve basic archetypes are reflected in the house meanings and in the aspects. This is abstract geometric design reiterated in multiple forms and combinations within astrological design.

Footnotes

1. Tobey, Carl Payne, Correspondence Course, Lesson 5, 1957, [no page numbers].
2. Ibid.
3. Ibid.
4. Tobey, Lesson 6.
5. Tobey, Lesson 7.
6. Ibid.
7. Ibid.

A Fresh View of House Rulership

There has been a raging debate over house rulership for the past 25 years since astrologer/academics like Robert Schmidt, Robert Hand, Robert Zoller, Benjamin Dykes, Robert Holden, etc. have been re-translating the texts of the Hellenistic Greeks and Medieval Arabs since the early 1990's. Actually the Brits have had this debate even longer since the late Olivia Barclay re-introduced Lilly in the 20th century. I remember going to a British AA conference in the summer 1994 and talking with some British astrologers that never used any planets beyond Saturn! And now so many astrologers have recently gone Vedic in their practices where they stop with Saturn.

All this has given rise to a renewed interest within our international astrological community in astrology's foundations and origins. As we attempt to ferret out the answers to the long debate about the function of houses versus signs. I have been closely following their findings since 1995. Now our global community is beginning a new debate on how to merge modern and traditional views into a post-modern astrology. As Rob Hand stated in 2005: "So we need to strike a balance between the modernist's attitude and the traditionalist's attitude."[1]

Deborah Houlding clearly states this dilemma in her revised her excellent book reviewing this debate in her 2006 edition of *The Houses, Temples of the Sky.* Robert Hand wrote the forward to the book and said:

> "It may ultimately be true that modern astrology has to go its own way in sorting out the houses. But let us at least do so, if we must, knowing that we have exhausted the possibilities of the old traditions. With this book I believe that there is no excuse for ignoring the history of the tradition."[2]

Houlding's book is a careful review of ancient and modern house meanings. She rejects the idea that there can be any association of sign rulership with the houses. She used the texts of Manilius, Firmicus, Al-Biruni, Lilly and Modern (she lumps all modern authors together) as comparisons of house meanings across time to show their consistency. Generally, during most of the 20th century, American astrologers followed the Aries house count of Aries ruling the first house, Taurus ruling the second house, Gemini to the third house, etc. until Pisces ruled the twelfth house.

Houlding said in her Introduction:

> "Since classical times houses have been one of the four essential components of astrology. Along with planets, signs and aspects, their 12-fold division of the celestial sphere forms a fundamental building block in astrological interpretation. Yet curiously, despite all the books that speak of the essential message of house meaning, very little existing contemporary literature to foster a true appreciation of that essence by illustrating where the meaning come from. The origin of their symbolism is poorly understood, and little effort has been made by modern astrologers to investigate and define their meaning... Within the contemporary theories of house meanings, there are presently only two that are given any real credibility. The first is a rather glib assumption that the houses are associated with, and take their meaning from, the signs of the zodiac... Traditional rulerships will fall by the wayside as they become inexplicable through the sign-originated theory... the signs were adapted and broadened out to incorporate the meaning of the houses, which correspond with their natural zodiacal order... The purpose of this book is to illustrate that none of the current theories on signs and psychological wheels can be regarded as historically correct, and that neither do they offer a full and reliable insight into the 'fundamentals' of house meanings which the astrologer relies upon in practical application."[3]

I agree with her conclusion that none of her references satisfy house rulership, **but she left out other ancient non-textual references and the American 20th century astrologer, Carl Payne Tobey.** The image below of the Goddess Nut, Mistress of the Sky whose image dates back to 200 AD has a strong, clear astrological message. This image is between the time of Manilius (10 AD) and Firmicus (4th century AD) which Houlding references. It is important to expand our astrological material beyond our fragmented multi-translated textual references. These other sources should be included in this new definition of post-modern astrology for the 21st century.

**The Goddess Nut,
British Museum**

I became a student of astrology in my college days. I once asked Dr. Sim Pounds, D.C. for an interview back in 1969. I was writing a research paper and there just wasn't much in astrology books available but I was allowed to do personal interviews. He was the President of the American Federation of Astrologers and by coincidence; he worked in my hometown of Tempe, Arizona. So I called him. He was too busy to give me the time but he suggested I call Carl Payne Tobey in Tucson, AZ. I did and the interview lasted all afternoon. I liked him so much he became my mentor in astrology.

Tobey had a completely different view on signs and houses from that of the majority of astrologers. He was part of a group of investigative New York City based astrologers in the 1930's and 40's that were trying to dissect astrology and understand its foundations. Sydney K. Bennett (aka Wynn) studied Sanskrit in order to read Indian texts. Grant Lewi was also part of this group. Tobey and Lewi were best friends. Others were Charles Jayne and Dane Rudhyar. They all socialized and published articles in the same magazines edited by Lewi. Lewi only used transits and he didn't use the Aries house count, he dropped all house rulerships. He just called the houses 'sectors' in his book, *Astrology for the Millions*.[4] Tobey was the resident statistician of the group. He gathered thousands of birthdates and hand calculated the data to prove basic principals long before there was a Michel Gauquelin. Tobey loved mathematics and pursued his study of number theory and geometry as his own personal interest. He was always trying to figure out the puzzle of the underlying foundation of astrological design. He firmly believed that astrology was a branch of geometry applied to life on Earth.

Fast-forward to 1993 when I decided to search the world for the clues supporting what Tobey had found by means of his own deductions and his 40+ years of experience. I was looking for the clues to the Tobey house/sign count. I was looking for patterns and images. I had done enough background study that I knew I could recognize and understand the astrological messages inherent in Egyptian images, if I could only find them. There is a great saying by Marcel Proust, *"The real voyage of discovery consists not in seeking new landscapes but in having new eyes."* Tobey certainly had new eyes with Uranus on his Sagittarius Ascendant. He was never a follower. He walked his own path.

The Egyptians were great geometers but their process did not include Arabic numbers, algebra or formulas. They used proportions, ratios and geometry. They had secret priesthoods that held their knowledge close to themselves, which the Greeks only partially understood. One of the great families of the Egyptian priesthood was named Petosiris. Some of our oldest astrological

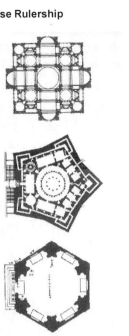

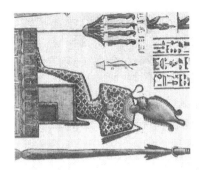

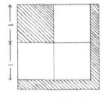

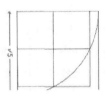

The throne upon which Osiris sits is clearly depicted as the square of 4, as it transforms into the square of 5 through the principle of √5 on which all the 0 proportions rest. It is therefore shown as the seat of the world of transformation through death and rebirth, represented by Osiris.

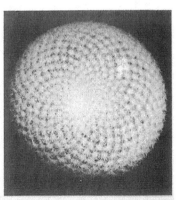

Seed distribution in a cactus plant which, as in the case of the sunflower, conforms exactly to the Golden Spiral.

Square Root of 5

The distribution of leaves around a central stem is governed by the Fibonacci Series: 3 leaves in 5 turns, 5 leaves in 8 turns.

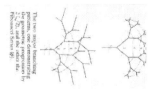

The two major branching patterns, one demonstrating the geometric progression by 2, 4, 8, and the other like Fibonacci Series (φ).

The Throne of Osiris

texts reference Petosiris.[5] The Tomb of Petosiris was shown in the prior chapter to demonstrate the Egyptian geometric knowledge prior to the Hellenistic Greeks. Unless you had knowledge of geometry, you would never guess the statue of Petosiris provide so much information.[6] Within it is the Golden Mean proportion based on the square root of 5 and **Phi**.

Another image that hides its geometric message is the Throne of Osiris that transforms the square of 4 into 5. It models the principal of *Phi* within it.[7]

By luck and synchronicity, I found in the Louvre gift shop, a French magazine *Archeologia*[8], with an astrological image, right there on the cover. The goddess of the sky Nut was painted on the inside lids of sarcophaguses so the dead could look up to the sky and see the realm of Nut's rulership.[9] The astrological signs are divided left and right and start with the signs of Leo and Cancer. The luminaries of the Sun and Moon rule only one sign each. Then the signs with co-rulerships run down her body in the Hellenistic planetary order of Mercury, Venus, Mars, Jupiter and Saturn.

In my prior chapter, I discussed that starting with the Egyptian New Year they assigned the Moon to Cancer, and the Sun to Leo, then Mercury to Virgo, Venus to Libra, etc. The Hellenistic Egyptians assigned planets to the astrological signs by **Average Mean Distance from Earth**.[10] The prior chapter was only half of the story of the astrological design represented in this image.

The division of the signs between Leo and Cancer is not arbitrary. Cancer/Moon on the right is lunar and represents the Egyptian New Year with the summer solstice at 0 Cancer. Leo/Sun on the left is solar so the element of duality is shown. There is a hidden message in this arrangement. The duality is representing the daily movement of the Earth's rotation against the sky. This is the same duality between the signs and houses represent by the division between Leo on the left and Cancer on the right. Another way to present this is to say that as we stand on the Earth, the vault of heaven is moving above us while Earth appears to be fixed. This daily motion shows the planets and signs rise from the eastern horizon and set in the west while the zodiacal houses stay fixed to the observer's location on Earth. The Egyptians placed great importance on the Sun being reborn every morning at sunrise and dying at sunset as the Goddess Nut swallowed the Sun. The Sun traveled down Nut's body during the night to be reborn the next morning. Note that the Egyptians were obsessed with the horizon at the Ascendant (sunrise) and the Descendant (sunset). They were constantly tracking the distance between the Sun and the horizon.

There is added meaning behind the image of the Sky Goddess

Nut with the Earth God Geb in coitus together. This is the duality of a rotating Heaven with a fixed Earth. They do a daily dance each day creating life on Earth. The duality of opposite motion splits the zodiac between Cancer and Leo. This structure is present in the meaning of the astrological signs and houses we use in astrology today. Daily motion creates the signs and houses as duality.

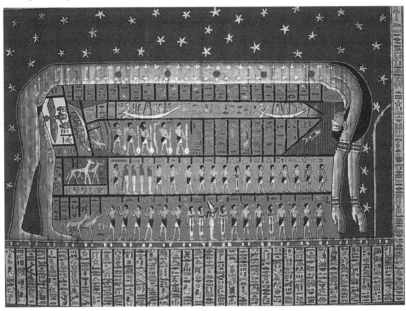

**Goddess Nut swallowing the Sun
to be reborn at Sunrise**

**The Earth God Geb with the
Sky Goddess Nut in Eternal Coitus**

We know the Egyptians carefully measured and tracked the astronomical movement of the Sun against the constellations. They maintained a soli-lunar calendar and a long Sothic calendar of 1,460 years for Sirius' heliacal rising cycle, not to mention planetary cycles too. The Egyptians were the masters of astronomy in the ancient world. There is a longer cycle of precession that is implied too with the division between Cancer and Leo. Robert Bauval in the Orion Mystery speculated that the Sphinx marked the 'First Time' of Tep Zepi when the constellation of Leo rose on the Spring Equinox around 10,500 BCE. This was repeated again during the Age of Taurus (at the Spring Equinox) when at that time the constellation of Leo was rising with the Summer Solstice at the Egyptian New Year and at the same time the Sun was entering the sign of tropical Cancer. This is an important historical era for the Egyptians to mark with monuments like the Pyramid of Giza since it married the conjunction of the constellation of Leo that marked the Egyptian 'First Time' and the Solar Disk of Ra to the Egyptian New Year. This precessional marking of time can be seen also with the Egyptian knowledge of the Ecliptic North Pole and the Geographic North Pole. Precession changes the star that marks the Geographic North Pole over time but the **Ecliptic North Pole is forever fixed and stationary at 0 Cancer.** The Egyptian New Year marked the highest elevation of the Sun in the Northern Hemisphere at the Tropic of Cancer which is also 0 Cancer. The Egyptians marked their country's boundary line at the First Cataract of the Nile on the Tropic of Cancer.

The Hellenistic period consisted of an amalgamation of concepts that have become our Western horoscopic astro-logy of today. This dual structure of opposite motion between Cancer and Leo is still present in the meaning of the astrological houses we use today in astrology.

The most common house meanings from tradi-tional sources according to Houlding are:[12]

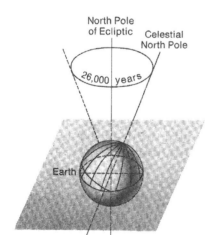

The precession of the equinoxes.

Ecliptic North Pole Forever Stationary at 0 Cancer[11]

Traditional Meaning and the Leo House Count

First House	Life, basic character, spirit, vitality, form and body shape, personality, outward behavior, success of enterprise	Leo & Sun
Second House	Livelihood, profit, fortune, gain, material possessions, wealth, substance, poverty, moveable goods, income, financial matters	Cancer & Moon
Third House*	Brothers and sisters, relatives, neighbors, short journeys, letters, rumors, messages, speech, communications	Gemini & Mercury
Fourth House	Father, parents, foundation of all things, real estate, family property, mining of metal, houses, tenements, farming, hidden treasure, family estates, fixed assets	Taurus & Venus
Fifth House	Children, pregnant women, pleasures, love affairs, plays, taverns, gaming, gambling, sport, risk taking, creativity	Aries & Pluto
Sixth House	Slaves, maids, servants and subordinates; infirmities and sickness, overwork, loss of property, small animals	Pisces & Neptune
Seventh House	Marriage, partnerships, open enemies, opposing party in love, war, quarrels or lawsuits	Aquarius & Uranus
Eighth House	Death, loss, Inheritance, expenditure, wills, income taxes, legacies, insurance, debts	Capricorn & Saturn
Ninth House*	Religion and clergy, knowledge, higher education, foreign lands, long journeys, divination, dreams, visions, philosophy	Sagittarius & Jupiter
Tenth House	Glory, distinction; honors, power, fame, career, reputation, absolute authority, professions, royalty, commanders, judges, authority, mothers, aspirations, social status	Scorpio & Mars
Eleventh House	Friends and acquaintances; clubs, fraternities and societies; hopes and desires; promotion by recommendation of friends; astrologers	Libra & Venus
Twelfth House	Places of confinement, hospitals, prisons, service, charity secret enemies, self-undoing, large cattle	Virgo & Mercury

* Whether the count starts with Aries or Leo, the 3rd and 9th house rulerships of Gemini and Sagittarius remain the same.

It has only been since the 20th century that astrological authors have assigned Aries to the first house, Taurus to the second house, Gemini to the third house, Cancer to the fourth houses, etc. This is a very new invention over the past 100 years. Lee Lehman states: "I have discovered that contemporary sources have completely obscured the essential differences between planet, sign and house. The concept that 1st House = Aries = Mars is mainly a modern invention"[13]

One influence to the Aries House assignments might be attributed to Evangeline Adams and Aleister Crowley, the ghost writer for her popular book, *Astrology, Your Place in the Sun* (1927).[14, 15] It is with this added confusion of the Aries house count that put Scorpio on the Eighth house, so sex was added to the Eighth house. Sex was never associated with the Eighth as Houlding clearly demonstrates.[16]   Other than minor attributes assigned to modern houses, the majority of house functions are basically intact from early writers. The Leo House Count fits perfectly with the traditional meanings, except there is confusion about the Sixth - Twelfth axis.

With the Leo House Count, the axis is of Pisces to the Sixth and Virgo to the Twelfth.   But in the Aries House Count the axis is Virgo to the Sixth and Pisces to the Twelfth. The signs are reversed between these two methods. These are the only two houses that are mixing up the principles of Pisces and Virgo. The function of these two houses need to be un-snarled and separated.

Twelfth House[17]
Firmicus: enemies, slaves, defects, illness, bad spirit.
Al-Biruni: enemies, misery, prison, fines, fear, disease, cattle, slaves, servant, exile
Lily: secret enemies, witches, self-undoing, imprisonment, horses, oxen elephants
Moderns: Seclusion, service, charity, unconscious, escapism, mysticism.

Sixth House[18]
Firmicus: infirmities and sickness
Al-Biruni: sickness, body defects, overwork, slaves, maids
Lily: sickness and disease, servants, labourers, small animals.
Moderns: work, subordinates, chores, health

We have various writers confusing health and sickness, work and subservience, secret enemies, fate and karma between these two houses. The karmic association comes from the Vedic tradition of associating the lunar nodes (which the Jyotish consider to be karmic) with the Twelfth House. This is not seen in the Hellenistic Greeks, they don't mention karma.

If one is sympathetic to the weaker, non-conformist elements of our social group, I would place that with Pisces. Musicians, artists, poets, psychics, mental illness, illegal drugs fit Pisces. If one is weak or ill, there is the need for servants and nurses to care for you. Non-conformity to rules, keeping secrets, having an underground associates would be with Pisces and the Sixth.[19] Tobey thought that Pisces was the best sign for being a spy and keeping secrets. This is the principle of the 'survival of the weak'. Pisces have empathy for the unfortunate, they want to help them. It is mass psychology and groupthink. It's the rhythm of the drums we count out with our feet and the chanting of a mantra to calm the mind and get the group into unison with drums of a tribal dance or a modern rock festival or rave.

If we assign Virgo to the Twelfth, it is the socially practical sign of Virgo that will build the institutions to house the non-conformists and the weak, like mental institutions, hospitals and prisons, all places of confinement.[20] But these are practical institutions that society builds to take care of people with problems. We separate the contagious from the healthy. We imprison the criminal to protect the social group. We build institutions to house the mentally ill or disabled. Pisces-Virgo doesn't kick the weak and abhorrent out of the tribe to die in the elements or to live as hermits. Virgo will build a place to institutionalize them, to protect the rest of us. It is a place of service to our social group. If one works as an employee, then that work is assigned to the Twelfth for work and service. These two houses badly need to be separated in functions.[21]

Our astrological community has been quite limited in that all the recent research of astrological history is constrained only to written texts. In other areas of study such as archeoastronomy, there has been a great emergence of our astrological history cloaked in words like shaman-priests (astrologers) and sky myths/ omens (astrological predictions). There is an avoidance of using the word 'astrology' but the research clearly reveals ancient temple alignments to stars and the layout of whole ancient cities with a purposeful design to create Heaven on Earth. We need to study and incorporate these astrological images that hold hidden information in our study of this very old practice and modern usage of Heaven on Earth. I know that this will disturb the traditionalists[22] **but I am attempting to bring in the ancient astronomical and geometric basis of how Hellenistic astrology was designed**. It will disturb some modern astrologers that are invested with Aries ruling the First House, but as Rob Hand said, "it's time to marry the modern with the traditional in order to have a functional whole for the 21st century."[23] The table above maintains all of the traditional house functions. The only exception is the Sixth and Twelfth but even these two are only changing which function belongs between them. Carefully look at the traditional list of house functions and see how well the Leo house count fits them like a glove.

I believe this is the correct rulership of the houses, a long debated issue that can be put to rest. This is the most logical explanation for the design behind the houses. I hope that open-minded people will investigate the truth in these discoveries. I have worked with this design for over 40 years and Tobey worked with it for another 50 years before me, along with his 700+ students. It functions well and gives a new perspective on the Sixth-Twelfth House issue.

Footnotes

1. Hand, Robert, *Towards a Post-Modern Astrology*, Astrological Conference 2005 of the British Astrological Association in York, UK. 2005, http://www.astro.com/astrology/in_postmodern_e.htm
    "So we need to strike a balance between the modernist's attitude and the traditionalist's attitude. By the way, I just want to make one thing clear: If I seem to be taking a slam at only certain members of the Jyotish/Vedic community in talking about astrological fundamentalism, believe me, I am not. There are also Lilly fundamentalists, Hellenistic fundamentalists, Arabic fundamentalists... You take any system, as long as it isn't modern, and you will find somebody who believes in it as a fundamentalist, or – to use a term more fashionable in religious circles – a *literalist, one who believes that the books are literally and completely true.*
    The modernist attitude believes that only the most recent work is any good, and the traditionalist attitude thinks that anything modern is hopelessly flawed and corrupt. Without qualification – these positions are both wrong. And if you disagree with me, fine. But that is my position, take it or leave it! (I have a Scorpio Moon)."

2. Houlding, Deborah, *The Houses, Temples of the Sky*, Wessex Astrologer, Bournemouth, England, 2006, Forward by Robert Hand.

3. Ibid, Introduction, p. x-xvii

4. Lewi, Grant, *Astrology for the Millions*, Llewellyn Publications, St.Paul, MN, 1969. P.26-27.

5. Houlding, p. 6

6. Lawlor, Robert, Sacred Geometry, Thames & Hudson Ltd., London 1982, p. 54-55

"The burial practices in the Pharaonic tradition were undertaken not merely to provide a receptacle for the physical body of the deceased, but also to make a place to retain the metaphysical knowledge which the person had mastered in his lifetime. The proportions of the seat of Petosiris as shown in his tomb reflect this intention."

7. Ibid. p.72
8. Desroches-Noblecort, Christiane "Le Zodiaque de Pharaon", Archelogia Numero 292, Juillet-Aout 1993, pages 21-45.
9. The sky-goddess Nuit, the mother both of Osiris, the god of death and resurrection, and Re, the sun-god (see Wells, 1992, 1993, 1994)... In Egyptian funerary texts, the coffin, tomb and sarcophagus of the pharaoh were themselves representations of the womb of the sky-goddess, within which his soul or spirit might begin the process of transformation and renewal. Such ideas surrounding the soul returning from whence it came, i.e. the womb of the cosmic mother, is echoed within various pre-dynastic burials, where the body of the deceased was laid to rest in a foetal position. see http://www.grahamhancock.com/forum/CollinsA2.php?p=1
10. *"Why Hellenistic Planetary Order?"* by Naomi Bennett, ISAR International Astrologer Journal, Vol 43, no 1, April 2014, p. 59-62.
11. Tompkins, Peter, *Secrets of the Great Pyramid*, p. 112 and 146.
12. Houlding is very thorough in her house meanings, but they are too extensive to list completely here.
13. Lehman, Lee. *Essential Dignities*, Whitford Press, 1989, p. 8.
    Crowley, Aleister, *The General Principles of Astrology*, edited by Hymenaeus Beta, Weiser Books, Boston, 2002 (originally 1927) p. 55.
14. In a conversation I had with Bernadette Brady in 2009 in Boston, she believed that Alan Leo was the source of the Aries House Count and that he was quite taken with Freud, but I have not been able to confirm this. It is a very recent 20th century invention.
15. Houlding, p.30.
16. Ibid, p. 54
17. Ibid, p. 55
18. Ibid, p. 58
19. Tobey, Carl Payne, *Astrology of Inner Space*, Omen Press, Tucson 1972, p. 173-77.

"Prisons seem definitely connected with Pisces and the Sixth House rather than the Twelfth, **but this might depend on whose viewpoint you were considering, that of the confined or that of those guarding them**. The Sixth House seems very definitely connected with health matters of one sort, while the twelfth is connected with another sort...

I always seemed to find the Sixth House...connected with weakness and a lack of spirit. As to servants, if you were strong enough to do your own work you wouldn't need them...I think the Sixth House is definitely connected to mental illness, and where paranoia is involved, this could include those secret enemies who are usually imaginary or self-created...

Pisces involves so much that you don't talk about. That's why its aspects make one so secretive...Attributing secret enemies to the Twelfth comes from associating that house with Pisces. I have never found any there, but I have found many people fearful of them because they were told that their planets in the twelfth house indicated they had dangerous secret enemies...Pisces is not in sympathy with so-called respectability. It goes around it secretly. Likely to have many strange associations...It should apply to the Sixth House, too. There is also compassion, sympathy for the underdog and the desire for reform."

20. Ibid, p.261.

"To me, the Twelfth is the house of work just as Virgo is the sign of work."

21. Ibid, p. 296-302.

"Virgo has been associated with medicines while alcohol, cigarettes, and all the illegal drugs are associated with the opposite sign, Pisces and its ruler, Neptune. Why should this line be drawn at this point? Some drugs are accepted by organized society and some are not. Virgo involves the accepted while Pisces is identified with the unacceptable...In the future marijuana may be included as acceptable...If Virgo turns sour and enters on a course of crime, as natives of all signs do at times, it seems to do a sophisticated kind of crime involving the falsification of records, forgery, counterfeiting, selling worthless stock, etc."

22. Houlding, introduction:

"The purpose of this book is to illustrate that none of the current theories on signs and psychological wheels can be regarded as historically correct, and that neither do they offer a full and reliable insight into the 'fundamentals' of house meanings which the astrologer relies upon in practical application. Its aim is to recapture the strength of the traditional perspective, where the astronomical and symbolic appreciation of spatial qualities is invested into the very core of our art..."

23. Hand, Robert, *Towards a Post-Modern Astrology*, Astrological Conference 2005 of the British Astrological Association in York, UK. 2005

Horoscope Construction and Aspects as Houses

There is a long history on horoscope measurements and construction resulting in more than a dozen ways to draw a chart in this modern day with quadrant houses. With the re-translations of the Greek texts at the end of the 20th century, this issue of which kind of house construction that is best for a horoscope is again at the forefront. Most of the Hellenistic Greeks used Whole Sign Houses where each house starts at 0 degrees and is a full 30 degrees wide. The Ascendant was calculated as a point in the whole sign first house. Ptolemy (100 AD) is not clear about his measurements of the houses or the Midheaven. The Greek texts have been re-translated multiple times so the Greek copies of copies are fragmented text and vague since Greek words have multiple meanings and the text is poorly written.[1] Two hundred years later, Firmicus Materus (300 AD) clearly used an Equal House system.[2] One could get lost in this debate of 'who wrote what and when' but let's add in the opinion of Dr. Livio Stecchini, who was an expert in ancient measurements and studied Hellenistic Greek knowledge. It was his firm opinion that the Hellenistic Greeks didn't understand the Egyptian measurements. Stecchini's opinion was:

"Stecchini's evidence shows that far from being the great innovators of geographical knowledge, the Alexandrine geographers of the next half millennium, such as Eratosthenes, Hipparchus and **Ptolemy were mainly handling and mishandling traditional data of an advanced science that preceded them, and which they only understood in part.**"[3]

Ptolemy didn't understand the difference between the Midheaven and the Nonagesimal. This is fundamental in the calculation of a horoscope because it mixes up ecliptic directions with geographic directions. This confusion about the ecliptic and geographic directions is the reason so many house systems are in use today. Below are three images from the Egyptians showing that they clearly understood the difference between the Geographic North Pole and the Ecliptic North Pole. Stecchini also said:

"In Stecchini's opinion, **the ancient Egyptians not only understood the precession of the axis of the earth but considered the true meridian the one passing through the pole of the ecliptic of the solar system.**"[4]

Hawk-headed man holding
a spear (pointing at the
Great Bear constellation) indicates the meridian through
the pole of the ecliptic,
according to Stecchini.

Ecliptic North Pole in the Great Bear [Nonagesimal][4]

The current mixing of geographic and ecliptic directions causes havoc for charts draw at high latitudes because the houses become distorted. All Table of Houses stopped at 66 degrees latitude because that is the Arctic or Antarctic Circle. This circle is just

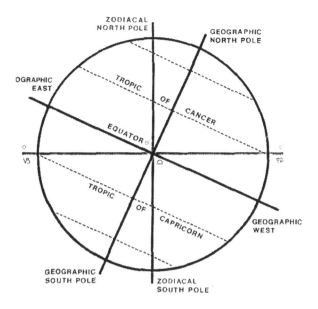

Ecliptic Poles vs. Geographic Poles at a 24 Degree Angle

another name for the Ecliptic North or South Pole. All house systems that use the Midheaven as the Tenth Cusp start to fail about this latitude.[5] See why in the diagram above.

The top vertical line is the Ecliptic (Zodiacal) North Pole but to its right is the Geographic North Pole. The Ascendant is drawn on the ecliptic line marked o Capricorn-o Cancer. It is perpendicular to the Ecliptic North Pole which is also the Nonagesimal, the Equal House Tenth Cusp. The Midheaven is drawn 24 degrees to the right from the Geographic North Pole. **How can one be at the Ecliptic North Pole walking zodiacally south while walking geographically north?** Geographic directions and ecliptic directions are 24 degrees apart. Look at the problem from above:

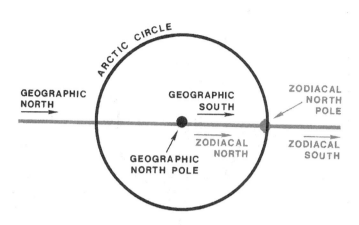

**View Above Earth Looking Down
at the Geographic North Pole**

This is why the house systems are messed up. They are measuring in two planes of space that are incompatible. A chart drawn in high latitudes with a Midheaven as the Tenth House Cusp looks like this:

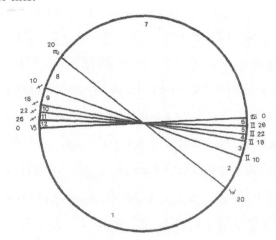

**A Chart Drawn with Midheaven Tenth Cusp
in High Latitude**

A simple solution for this problem is to calculate a horoscope using the Equal House System. There is no mix up of geographic and ecliptic directions. This is the same chart using equal houses:

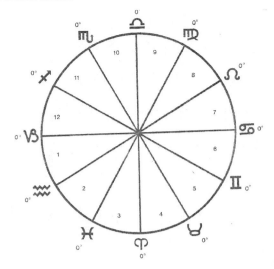

Same Chart Drawn with Nonagesimal Tenth Cusp
in High Latitude

The simple solution for the Midheaven is to put it in a chart as a point, just like a planet, Arabic part or lunar node. This preserves the Midheaven and all aspects to the Midheaven and the chart is drawn correctly.

It has been only in the last several hundred years that charts have been drawn in the round. Most medieval astrologers drew their charts as squares. The Jyotish astrologers still do.

In both square horoscopes, the houses are drawn as triangles with the cusps being at the apex of each house. This is a very different concept in the house structure where the cusp is in the middle of the triangle versus the round horoscope having the cusp drawn as the beginning of the house.[6]

It is my contention that the cusp is the center of the house and that the house extends 15 degrees on either side of the cusp. This was proven to be true by Michel Gauquelin of France with his massive statistical study of profession and birth charts. Prominent planets fell into the Twelfth house and the Ninth house. This corresponds well with the concept of the apex as the center of a house. At the bottom of the following page is an image of Gauguelin's famous study of the placement of Mars for professional athelitcs.[7] Note the massing of data above the Ascendant into the twelfth house and a second high massing past the Tenth cusp into the Ninth house. This corresponds to the idea of a house cusp is an apex, that is the center of a house.[8]

Medieval Square Chart

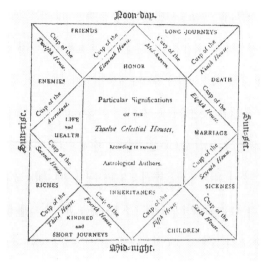

Jyotish Square Chart

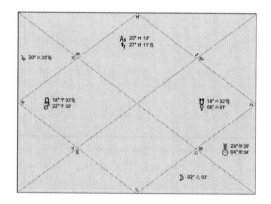

The Mars Effect for Athletics Against Circular House Cusps

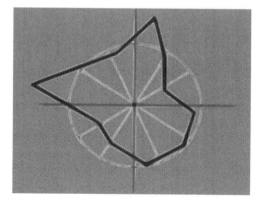

One favorite chart I will use to compare the Nonagesimal against the Midheaven chart is that of Charles, Prince of Wales. Look at the difference between the Equal House chart and the Midheaven chart. London is relatively high latitude so there a distortion of the house size at 50 degrees latitude.

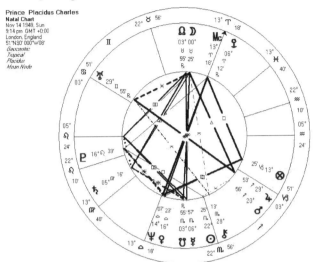

Prince Charles with proportional Placidus Houses
Midheaven/Tenth Cusp at 13 Aries

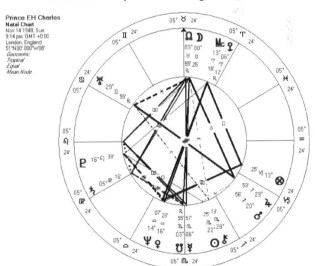

Prince Charles with Equal Houses and
Nonagesimal Tenth Cusp

I won't analyze the entire chart since this is an example of the calculation on the Tenth Cusp that represents career, accomplishment, honors, reputation, prominence or parent with authority, sometimes the mother. The Nonagesimal is conjunct the North Node and Moon and opposing it is Mercury, the planet of work and service on the Fourth Cusp. Which chart fits him better? He has spent his entire life in waiting for his elevation to King of England. It has been the need of the Crown (his mother/Moon) for him to marry properly and the demand of the Royal Family that made him marry Diana. His entire career has been in the service of the family assets. He fulfills his royal responsibilities that are pure Fourth/Tenth cusp duty and obligation to the family and his mother. He was again marked after the death of Princess Diana when he married the love of his life, Camilla. Now look at his chart surrounded by the chart of his mother, Elizabeth II, Queen of the United Kingdom.

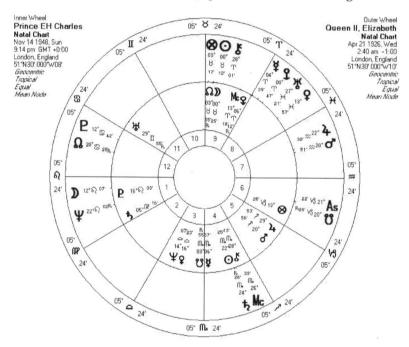

**Inner Wheel is Prince Charles,
Outer Wheel is Queen Elizabeth II**

The Queen's Sun is conjunct Charles' Moon and on the Nonagesimal! What a re-enforcement of the Tenth Cusp! She holds his career in her hands. To me, the Equal House chart reflects his public life being dominated and defined by the women around him much more than the Midheaven chart.

The Whole Sign chart will not display this prominence as well only because the power aspects to the Ascendant are not clearly shown. It is up to the astrologer to remember to look for aspects to the Ascendant. The use of Whole Signs isn't a problem if the Ascendant is in the middle of a sign but if it is near 27 degrees or 3 degrees, then the house cusps are distorted. I see the Equal House chart as a refinement of the Whole Sign houses. In the ancient past it was difficult to determine the degree on the Ascendant or to know the birth time within an hour. With better measurements and the recording of birth times, the Ascendant became accurate down to the degree and now the minute. It is the ecliptic degree on the eastern horizon at birth that is all-important. It defines the cardinal axis of the First, Fourth, Seventh and Tenth cusps. The horoscope may have started out as Whole Sign but with modern accuracy, I prefer the Equal House chart. If the time of day is not known, then I put the chart's Sun on the First Cusp. This makes every cusp point an aspect to the Sun as a Solar chart. The Ascendant is a major point in a horoscope and **all house cusps are angular aspects to the Ascendant**. If the Sun's position is used for an Ascendant than all house cusps are aspects to the Sun. If a derived chart is created with the Part of Fortune (Part of the Moon), then all house cusps are aspects to the Part of Fortune. Note the importance of geometric angle is again being used with an Ascendant or a derived point.

Out-Of-Sign-Aspects, Aspects as Houses

The Hellenistic Greeks also believed that out-of-sign aspects did not function. For example, if Mars is at 29 Aquarius and Saturn is at 1 Gemini, the Greeks did not consider these two planets were square (90 degrees) each other because Mars is out-of-sign (not in Pisces yet) so the two planets cannot be in square. Yet by a modern viewpoint the squaring aspect is functional and forming within two degrees, almost exact! When Project Hindsight had a Traditions List in the late 1990's there was a flame war at one point. It was during a transit of Mars opposing Uranus, out-of-sign. Within two days of this out-of-sign aspect completely forming, the list moderators of Robert Schmidt and Robert Hand took down the Traditions List and terminated it. I wrote Rob Hand pointing out that the termination occurred during an out-of-sign opposition that the Greeks claimed didn't work!

The Greeks also claimed the signs next to each other could not be in aspect, that the two signs 'could not see each other.' This would be the 30-degree aspect and also the 150-degree aspect. I don't find this to be true and neither did Tobey. I primarily use only 30-degree multiples of aspects but many modern astrologers use the 45-degree and 135-degree aspects that were created by Kepler. These are weaker versions of the 90-degree square aspect. Tobey, in his astrological discoveries of geometric design in astrology created the pattern below of **aspects associated with zodiacal houses using the Leo House Count of ruling signs to the houses.**

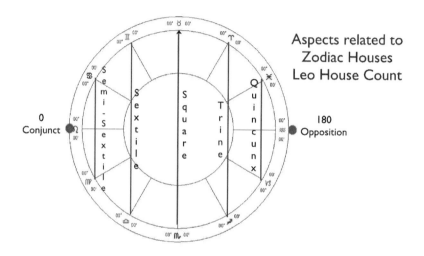

Aspects Assigned to Houses with Leo House Count

This assignment of house rulership to aspects makes sense when we look at the traditional Ptolemic aspects which are:

0-degree	Conjunction	Positive and Creative
60-degree	Sextile	Communicative and Social
90-degree	Square	Difficult, Limiting and Frustrating
120-degree	Trine	Expansive, Positive, Fortunate
180-degree	Opposition	Change, Endings and Beginnings

The pattern that is created looks like:

0-degree	Conjunction	Leo/Sun **Future Fire** Individual Drive
60-degree	Sextile	Gemini/Mercury with Libra/Venus **All Future Air**, Family and Social Intelligence
90-degree	Square	Taurus/Venus with Scorpio/Mars **All Past** with Family Survival
120-degree	Trine	Aries/Pluto with Sagittarius/Jupiter **All Future Fire**, Family and Social Drive
180-degree	Opposition	Aquarius/Uranus **Future Air** Individual Intelligence

To complete this pattern, there are two more 30-degree aspects of the 30-degree Semi-Sextile and the 150 degree Quincunx. The Greeks ignored these aspects but modern astrologers find them functional.

30-degree	Semi-Sextile	Cancer/Moon with Virgo/Mercury **All Past** Individual and Social Survival
150-degree	Quincunx	Pisces/Neptune with Capricorn/Saturn **All Past** Social and Individual Survival

Tobey considered the Semi-Sextile to represent weakness and lack of energy. It is associated with two past signs that represent fear of survival and conforming to social conventions or getting mired in the details. The Quincunx is about the past with the incompatibility of nebulous Pisces/Neptune with concrete, defined Capricorn/Saturn. These two signs are like mixing oil and water. They will not blend, they don't relate to each other. This aspect is associated with only partial adherence to the rules, illness and weakness.

It appears at this writing in August 2014 that Robert Hand has the beginning of the same idea as Tobey. The Mountain Astrologer Magazine interviewed him for it's Sept/Oct 2014 issue (a revised *Planets in Transit* book is coming out 2015) and he states:

"Yes, I'm addressing the issue of aspects being a form of house relationships. For example, sextiles are 3rd-house and 11th-house aspects, which means they impinge on things that the 3rd and 11th houses impinge on, in a more general way. The houses are much more specific. **But I think the aspects and the houses all arise out of the sign relationships**."

This is exactly the same discovery Tobey made more than 60 years ago. Perhaps the merging of modern and traditional astrology is getting closer.

Footnotes

1. Hand, Robert "An Interview with Robert Hand, the Integration of Modern and Traditional Astrology", *The Mountain Astrology Magazine*, Oct/Nov. 2014.
    "frankly, none of these astrologers succeeded in going back to Ptolemy, because somewhere in their heart of hearts, they realized that was impossible. If you go back to Ptolemy, you don't have a functioning system of astrology! The Tetrabiblos is not a complete text. It's a combination of a critique of earlier methods and a basic text, but it is not a complete text. For example, houses are hardly mentioned at all, and certainly you get no idea what to do with them. Even aside from that, the 1st-century astrologer Dorotheus of Sidon seems to have had more influence on the Arabs than Ptolemy did, at least on a practical level, so when the later 16th- and 17th-century astrologers tried to purge the tradition of material they thought was from the Arabs, they were actually removing much of the remaining material from the early Hellenistic tradition...
    The quadrant houses, in some form or other, may have a future, as I have mentioned, particularly regarding the quantitative intensity of a planet. I do not think they have a future as an indication of signification, however. If they do, someone had better come up with a theoretical justification. But even then, **we still have the main theoretical problem that has dogged all of us from Rhetorius forward, which is: Which quadrant house system?**"
2. Schmidt, Robert. "House Division, Planetary Strength, and Cusps in Hellenistic Astrology." This is in the introduction to Book III of the Tetrabiblos translated by Robert Schmidt for Project Hindsight, with the permission of Keith J. Williams of the Traditions Mail List. 1997
    "In the midst of all this confusion, and assuming that Valens does have in mind some system of equal zodiacal division based on the Ascendant degree, let me make a speculation based on **Valens' use of lot which may provide us with an important clue about the relationship between whole-sign houses and equal divisions from the**

Ascendant. It is intrinsic to his treatment of lots that they may be regarded as "Horoskopoi," or quasi-ascendants; that is, they can become the first houses of derivative whole-sign systems, the meanings of these signs in succession being analogous to those in the basic natal chart. The only real difference is that the fundamental whole-sign system is regarded as more general, while the derivative system is intended to yield greater detail. Nevertheless, they are conceptualized in the same way.

Now, the lot itself occupies a degree somewhere in the sign destined to become the first house of a derivative system; the presence of the lot must be thought of as somehow altering the very sign in which it falls, making it an appropriate first house for that of which it is the lot (the father, for instance). **Similarly, the sign in which the Ascendant degree falls becomes the first house of the general whole-sign arrangement; the Ascendant degree is a <u>kentron, a pivot or hinge</u> around which the sign turns, and it is this pivoting that alters the sign and makes it serve the role as the first whole-sign, wherever the Ascendant point may fall in the sign itself.** Might not the first degree of each equal "house" from the Ascendant be regarded as the "pivot" of the whole-sign in which it occurs, a kind of point around which it turns and which makes the entire sign the second place (or house), for instance, giving it its unique character? Thus, the "twelve-turning" would be an extension of the idea of a pivot, formerly restricted to the angles, to all the intermediate signs...

It is interesting to note that **Maternus is the first author we know of who explicitly uses an equal house system from the Ascendant** (in Book II, chapter 19, even though he elsewhere uses whole-sign places relative to the Ascendant, as in Book III, chapter 2). **He is two hundred years after Ptolemy and Valens...**

Ptolemy's Equal House System

Ptolemy is regarded as the author of a special equal house division that begins five degrees above the Ascendant, and it is now widely assumed that this was his preferred system. However, three things need to be pointed out here. First of all, prior to Book III, chapter 11, the discussion of length of life, there is no reason to believe that Ptolemy regards the Horoskopos, Midheaven, etc., as anything other than whole-sign houses. He uses all the traditional language of pivots, post- ascensions, and declines.

And from the number of manuscript variations at key points in the text, **it appears that a number of readers and copyists were in doubt on exactly this issue. I should further mention that all these house names**

are so loosely connected to the basic syntax of the sentence that they could even have been interpolated by a later editor...

We invite modern astrologers to try to distinguish these two aspects of house division in their chart readings."

3. Tompkins, Peter, *Secrets of the Great Pyramid*, Harper and Row, New York, 1971, p. 214-215.

"In his reconstruction of pre-classic geographical data, Stecchini has traced an advanced science of geography based on accurate astronomical tables which were kept up to date all the way down to the beginning of the first millennium BC. He has established that the later Babylonians still had excellent maps for their area of the world between the 30th and 36th parallels, made in segments of 6 degrees latitude by 7 degrees 12 minutes of longitude, which gave them perfect squares because of the diminished length of a degree of longitude between those parallels.

This same system says Stecchini, was in use as late as the reign of Darius the Great of Persia, whose empire, centered on the arbitrary geodetic point of Persepolis, ran precisely 3 units of 7 degree 12 minutes East of the Egyptian meridian and three units of 7 degree 12 minutes west of the Indian border. But errors were already creeping into the geography because of a lack of direct observation of celestial phenomena and because of the reliance by geographers on ancient astronomical data that were no longer up to date.

As an explanation for this regression of geographic science, especially during the Hellenistic period, and therefore almost to modern times, Stecchini suggests that when Alexander the Great destroyed Persepolis in the 4th century BC he may have exterminated the Egyptian geographers imported by the Persians to do their figuring, and that when he dismantled the center of Egyptian science at Heliopolis in order to build his own capital at Alexandria, he may have compounded the damage*

*Heliopolis, the On of the Bible, was considered the greatest university in the world. It had existed since much earlier times under the domination of the priests, of whom there were said to be 13,000 in the time of Rameses III, 1225 BC. More than 200 years earlier, Moses was instructed at Heliopolis 'in all the wisdom of the Egyptians,' which included physics, arithmetic, geometry, astronomy, chemistry, geology, meteorology and music.

The destruction of Persepolis and Heliopolis were considered by Alexander essential in order to destroy the geographic, and therefore the political, basis of the older empires.

Stecchini's evidence shows that far from being the great innovators of geographical knowledge, the Alexandrine geographers of the next half millennium, such as Eratosthenes, Hipparchus and **Ptolemy were mainly handling and mishandling traditional data of an advanced science that preceded them, and which they only understood in part.**"

4. Ibid., p. 174.

"According to Zaba this line held by the hawk-headed man indicates the meridian through our [geographic] north pole. But Professor Livio Stecchini points out that Zaba did not notice that this line always ends at a very specific position, at times with an arrow point, which divides the seven stars of the Great Bear into four and three. This line, says Stecchini, does not indicate the meridian passing through the north point, but the meridian passing through the pole of the ecliptic. In Stecchini's opinion, **the ancient Egyptians not only understood the precession of the axis of the earth but considered the true meridian the one passing through the pole of the ecliptic of the solar system**. Lockyer added that the Babylonians had distinguished the pole of the equator from the pole of the ecliptic, naming the former Bil and the latter Anu.

This evidence leaves little doubt that the ancient Egyptians knew there were two poles in the sky, a [ecliptic] north pole, which shifted round a fixed [geographic] pole, or 'open hole' in the heavens; they also knew that this slow circling brought about the precession of the equinoxes."

5. Technical articles on various house systems and how a chart is drawn can be found on the Uranian Trust website by Graham Bates, "Charts Are Not Flat" 2012. There are several articles by Michael Wackford at: http://www.skyscript.co.uk/polar5.html

6. Hand, Robert, "A Study in Early House Division," *The Astrological Association Journal*, London July 1997.
http://www.astrologer.com/aanet/pub/journal/jojul97.html

"We tend to think of cusp as meaning beginning. But this is not its correct meaning. **A cusp (Latin cuspis) is a point with the clear implication of apex rather than beginning.** For example, our bicuspid teeth have two peaks or points, not two beginnings.

Could it be that a cusp is simply a point that has the strongest quality associated with the house and that it could fall anywhere within a house? We have a well-established convention even in modern astrology (although many moderns are not aware of it) that a house begins approximately five degrees before the cusp...

And the Ascendant is not the only place that can make a sign a first house or place. For certain purposes various planets can do this, and most of the Lots (which we call erroneously "Arabic Parts") also mark signs as being first places of derived house systems..."

For what we do not see in Valens is houses being counted from the Midheaven. We only explicitly see the sign of the Midheaven doing double duty as a tenth and ninth house or sign...

How do we compute the intermediate cusps? This is the major problem of modern house division and nothing here solves it...

But at least we do see another instance, perhaps, of how the early astrologers dealt with signs as houses even as they were making a transition to the modern modes of dealing with houses as zones demarcated by the cusps."

7.   http://astrologynewsservice.com/articles/the-gauquelin-controversy/

"Michel Gauquelin was a graduate in statistics and psychology from the Sorbonne who, together with his wife Francoise, conducted the most significant body of statistical research in astrology to date. While his work does not substantiate some canons of traditional astrology, it conclusively vindicates astrology's fundamental premise: that there is a relationship between the planets' positions at the moment of birth and the direction of individual lives.

The body of Gauquelin's work extends over a period of 23 years (1949 –1973) and involved research into questions of professional studies, heredity studies and character trait studies. By far the studies receiving the most notoriety involved correlations between the position of a planet in the natal chart and a person's chosen profession. Because of its extremely significant positive results, the most famous of these studies is commonly known as "the Mars effect."

8.   Hand, magazine interview, *The Mountain Astrologer Magazine*, Oct/Nov. 2014.

"For example, take Whole Sign houses when applied to the Gauquelin results. If you add two postulates, two assumptions, to the definition of angularity, which are that a planet must be (a) in the rising sign and (b) if it's below the Ascendant, to be as close to it as possible, and if you do the same with the Midheaven, then you get the Gauquelin sectors. Because, as the rising sign rises, the angular planets will tend to be above the horizon, which is just starting to rise. They have to be close to the horizon to be powerful. And there's another study that needs to be done: It may be possible that, if we separate out the people whose dominant planets are in the actual signs of the angles (not the 10th house but the Midheaven house), we may find the results significant there, too."

Reliable Predictions

Astrology has proven itself with character interpretation of individuals and event descriptions but the great challenge is, can we predict the future? This has been a continuing challenge and problem for astrology. Currently we have very accurate computer software to calculate horoscopes and very accurate ephemerides to predict the location of planets in the future or look backwards to prior locations. This was not always the case.

In the ancient past, it was hard to know the hour of birth or to calculate the exact degree rising on the horizon. They guessed at the degree of the planets during the Greek period or used out of date planetary tables[1] that were calculated for a different location. Local time was from water clocks or sundials, getting a time was close if it was within an hour. Could the horizon be seen to see what was on the Ascendant? Observations were made and recorded but only for what had passed. Birth charts were delayed by many months to ensure that an infant would survive. The first measuring instrument was an astrolabe[2] around 150 BC. More improvements were made by the Arabs with a better astrolabe and the revision of the planetary tables to make them accurate again. But it wasn't until 1670 that Kepler's three laws of planetary motion[3] was widely accepted and new planetary tables were calculated with accuracy that the future position of planets could be calculated.[4]

Before accurate planetary tables, many methods were used for prediction, such as Hellenistic time lords, progressions (secondary, tertiary, contra, Naibod), solar arc directions, planetary periods of Egyptian Terms or Chaldeans Terms, or 43 different kinds of dasas (Jyotish planetary periods).[5] None of these give the accuracy of transits yet they linger on in modern astrology to this day. It is part of the tradition that needs serious revision. There are so many variations of each of these techniques that it could take a lifetime to cross analyze these to see which ones work better.

Progressions, Directions, Planetary Periods

Of the ancient methods still in use today, it is a common belief today that progressions or planetary periods are necessary for transits to produce an event. I do not find that is necessarily true. The belief that three aspects are necessary for an event to occur is probably correct, but those aspects can be all transits to natal positions. There is no need for progressions to be used too. There are a few prominent astrologers in the past who have stated that progressions don't work because they generally have suffered much backlash and criticism from others so they quietly just don't use them.

Raphael (R.T. Cross, the 7th Raphael (1850-1923) in 1901 stated: "The stern facts of life do not bear out such copious influences, and it is practically a waste of time to work out the Primaries, as they are called, when not more than 10 per cent will be found to coincide with an event. I regret I must adhere to the opinion so often expressed, which, that none of our systems of Directions are correct"[6]

Sydney K. Bennett (Wynn) dropped them in the late 1920s after a near fatal accident in Merced, California when he thought he was under very fortunate progressions.[7] Grant Lewi just quietly never used them. As editor for three major astrology magazines from the 1930's to the 1950's, he had seen the backlash to Bennett's public denial of progressions. He was a bit of a politician navigating the public needs of his peers, so he never stated a public opinion. He simply said he used transits.[8]

Since Carl Payne Tobey was a close friend of Sydney K. Bennett and Grant Lewi, he gave up progressions very early in his astrological career. He stated his strong opinion against progressions only in his private lessons to students. He left his mind open to progressions but never used them with clients and said to his students: "Coming back to progressions, our conclusion is that they are inaccurate."[9]

In general, much caution must be taken in the use of progressions and various planetary periods. They are too unreliable to confidently use with clients. As a student of astrology, they are worth studying but transits are the most reliable technique that can be utilized with clients.

Transits

I consistently use the graphic ephemeris of 90 degrees since it plots out all hard aspects to the natal chart. It is the hard aspects of conjunctions, squares and oppositions that have the most reliable results in events or situations. Looking for the combination of transiting Sun or transiting Mars to long term hard transits point to a crisis or event culmination when issues come to an apex. The image below is a 90-degree graph of Putin's natal chart (symbols down the right side of the graph) plotted with 2014 transits. It shows that the Grand Cross transit in April was affecting his Sun and a cluster of

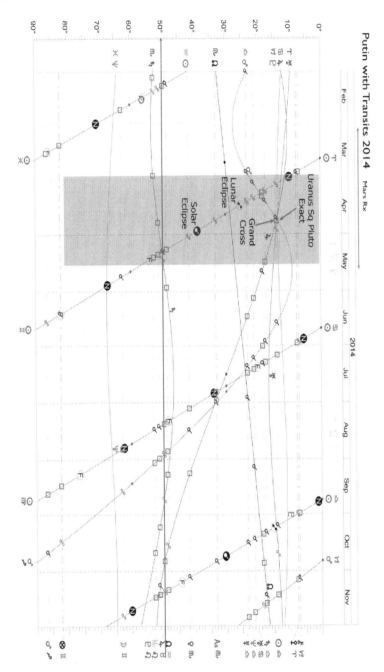

Putin's Natal Chart with 2014 Hard Aspect Transits

his planets in the Cardinal signs. With these I was predicting his military aggression continuing with Ukraine until the end of June 2014 because transiting Mars was retrograding and would not clear these positions until the end of June 2014. As of this writing, that was the case. It is likely that a resolution to Ukraine will not happen until after April 2015.

The 60-degree graph is utilized for most soft aspects of the conjunction, sextile and trine. These are events that emphasize communication, the power of friendships and association, and creative opportunities that advance events into the future with ease. I use this graph if the client wants to meet new people or start a creative project. These transits require action on the part of the client to get results otherwise they can pass unnoticed.

Solar Returns

Solar Returns are a form of transits that many astrologers use for predictions. The Solar Return chart was first used by Abū Ma'shar (778-886 in Iraq). It is a snapshot of an event chart set exactly to the degree and minute of the Sun's return to its natal place each year on the client's birthday. That can mean that the SR chart has a different ascendant every year and it takes 33 years for the SR Ascendant to go around the zodiac. The placement of the Ascendant, Sun and Moon in the SR chart are considered important. Many astrologers recommend that a client travel to a location that improves the SR chart for the coming year. But others think this is unnecessary and irrelevant since the client will spend the majority of the year in their home city and only a day or so in the relocated city. Lee Lehman is a nationally known astrologer and she reviews the history of solar returns and the use of them by herself and other current astrologers in her book *Classical Solar Returns*.[10] In a private email to me in 2013 she stated: "I work with solar returns and transits. I do see value in the progressed lunation cycle, and I'm not saying that progressions don't "work," but they also don't pop in the way I'd like to see."

Before the time of personal computers, solar returns were an improved technique for predictions and many astrologers used it because it minimized the amount of time it took to do predictions for the coming year (which could take many hours). However, now that we can get personalized printouts of transits against a client's chart in minutes, not hours. Why use this shortcut? It is a moment in time representing an entire year. I seriously question its accuracy versus the use of transits to see the entire year with its general trends and peak periods plotted out on a graph. Most astrology software programs can even advance transits against a natal chart and step it forward in time or backwards so that the house placements can be viewed too. I find the use of transits across the year to be consistently more accurate.

Planetary Nodes

Another important factor in predictions is the tracking of the transiting lunar nodes across a natal chart. Major life events and surprising turns in events can happen when an eclipse (solar or lunar) is in hard aspect (conjunct, opposition or square) to major points in a natal chart. In general the order of importance for an eclipse event to a natal position would be Ascendant, Sun, Moon, Mars, and Venus. A natal Midheaven can have a strong eclipse transit if the natal Midheaven is strongly aspected by other planets. I have found that transiting aspects that square the Ascendant/ Descendant are far stronger and more consistent than any transits to a Midheaven (unless the Midheaven has hard aspects natally). I notice transits can generate events consistently with the equal house 10th or 4th House, but rarely with the Midheaven. So, I practice caution in making predictions with the Midheaven, especially with charts drawn for high northern latitudes.

There are planetary nodes that can be quite important for predictions and natal characteristics. Nodes always come in pairs since the nodes mark the place where a planet crosses the ecliptic. There is always a north node and a south node that are 180 degrees apart. When a planet moves north across the ecliptic, it is called a north node. When the same planet moves south across the ecliptic, it is called the south node.[11]

Nationally known 20th century American astrologers such as Grant Lewi, Carl Payne Tobey, Dane Rudhyar, Charles Jayne and Michael Erlewine have extensively used the planetary nodes. I use the heliocentric planetary nodes as having the same energy as the actual planet. These heliocentric planetary nodes act as if the physical planet was in hard aspect to a natal position or transits. They are hidden modifiers that need to be considered in delineations. These nodes are best used with only hard aspects but the strength of the square aspect is cut in half. Square aspects don't have the same power as conjunctions or oppositions. A limited orb for the planetary nodes of one degree for Mercury, Venus and Jupiter is best. A 1.5 degree orb can be used for Mars, Saturn, Uranus or Pluto. I don't use them in chart analysis unless they make hard aspects to important natal planets or a cardinal house cusp.

Planet	North Node 2010	North Node 2000	North Node 1900	Annual Movement
Mercury	18TA 27'54"	18TA 20'48"	17TA10'48"	42.6"
Venus	16GE46'52"	16GE41'28"	15GE45'36"	32.4"
Mars	19TA48'59"	19TA44'22"	18TA57'22"	27.7"
Jupiter	10CN35'31"	10CN28'24"	9CN28'12"	36.7"
Saturn	23CN43'39"	23CN38'25"	22CN47'05"	31.4"
Uranus	14GE02'24"	13GE59'24"	13GE29'24"	18.0"
Neptune	11LE53'05"	11LE46'31"	10LE40'51"	39.4"
Pluto	20CN26'49"	20CN18'41"	18CN57'21"	48.8"
Eris	06TA12'	06TA07'	04TA21'	30.0"

Declinations and OOB (Out of Bounds) Planets

I use both of these techniques when there are hard aspect transits already in place, and then declination can become important or emphasize the energy of the hard aspect. Angular aspects in astrology are given in ecliptic longitude. But a planet has latitude also. How far above and below is the planet from the equator? Are two planets visibly conjunct in the sky? They could be in the same ecliptic degree but separated in the sky vertically. Their intensity will increase if they sit vertically and horizontally together in the sky that is called parallel. Tobey said he did use parallel declinations but he didn't get much from contra-parallel planets. Contra-parallel is when two planets are equally distant from the equator but one is north and the other is south of the equator.

Out of Bound (OOB) planets were first discussed and named by Kt Boehrer in 1994.[12] It's a well-observed modern concept that has received much recognition by other astrologers. The concept is that when a planet's declination exceeds the Tropic of Cancer or the Tropic of Capricorn (ecliptic inclination of 23 degrees 26 minutes from the equator) the characteristic behavior of the planet becomes erratic and unconventional in astrological terms. This is especially true of the Moon and Mars. These are the two planets with the strongest association of erratic, extreme behavior for natal personality analysis and some event charts. Boehrer used 31 charts from Dr. Harry Darling of known patients with mental illness. Twenty of the 31 charts had OOB planets and of those 31 charts, six had OOB Mars and 8 had multiple OOB planets. Boehrer states:

"The most striking feature of the chart with one or more planets out-of-bounds is the tremendous energy demonstrated in the individual. We find that those born with natal out-of-bounds planets are high achievers, even over achievers...The other side of the coin, naturally, is the realization that this tremendous energy may become uncontrollable or may be misused. In such cases the potential for destructive action is devastating and the contrasting potential of the OOB planets would seem to prove the old bromide that 'genius hovers on the edge of madness' is, in fact, a great truth."[13]

Steven Forrester describes OOB Moon thus: "Of all the planets, the Moon is most dramatic in it effects when Out of Bounds, in my experience. In fact of all the astronomical loose ends that are basically ignored in mainstream astrological practice, this Out of Bounds Moon is one of the most astonishing in its repercussions... The Out of Bounds Moon is spontaneous, emancipated, liberated, released in its own recognizance, and utterly on its own."[14]

I have found only one book on OOB natal planets by a psychiatrist, Mitchell E. Gibson, M.D.[15] He is not an astrologer in the conventional sense. He plotted angular aspects of planets and declinations on an X-Y graph, not a horoscope. He found a direct correlation between mental illness and OOB planets, especially the Moon, Mars and Saturn. He also extended the use of OOB (he renamed it Exdek) to include high declinations between 21-23 degrees, which he called Hidek. He found a high correlation of major depression with OOB Mars and Saturn. Notice the X-Y graph with Mars conjunct Saturn in Hidek as one example of an individual. It's a perfectly good way to chart a natal horoscope with declinations. House divisions could have been added easily.[16]

I was lucky to have an astrological mentor in Carl Payne Tobey. He wanted his students to be open to observation and to make their own critical correlations between events and astrology. There are many beliefs, techniques and astrological lore that are repeated and maintained in this tradition that may or may not be true. Tobey encouraged critical thinking and independent observation, as did Grant Lewi. This is still needed today. There is now astrological software that can calculate every technique under the sun, but which are important and relevant to an event or natal chart? It is easy for a student to get confused and lost in all of the choices. That is why it is so important to be a critical observer. I believe it is best to use only the most reliable technique of transits for several years of study

Major Depression

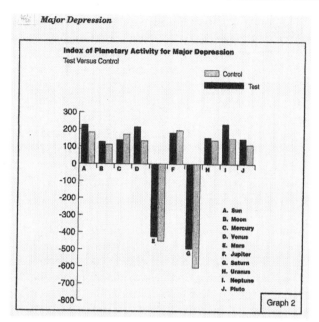

Depression Plotted with Planets

Major Depression

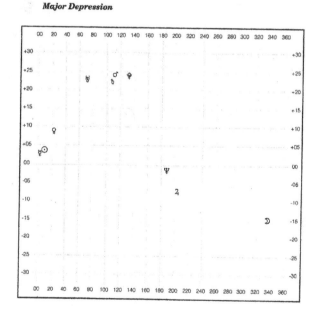

Planets Charted by Degree and Declination on a Grid

and observation before adding other factors that do not have the same consistency. This will lower the confusion of what is actually effective.

Watch national and local news events with an eye on current transits. From October 2012 to December 2014, Saturn has transited in Scorpio. There were a series of global events regarding rape (sex and Scorpio) in the American military and trying to change the rules (Saturn) on how to handle the chain of command for reporting this abuse. India dealt with global attention of gang rape of women. There were two major USA news events of Secret Service agents going to prostitutes in South America, the release of sexual captives in the US and a yearlong news event of South African Oscar Pistorius' trial (Saturn consequences) of murdering his girlfriend on Valentine's Day 2013. He is the world renowned Blade Runner who loves guns and has a short temper. It has been written in news reports that he was a jealous and insecure boyfriend. He was reported to have shot a gun in a restaurant and asked his friend to take the rap in 2013. He was also seen shooting a gun out of a car's sunroof after an incident with a police officer.[17]

When I follow the transit of Saturn, I look for the addition of hard aspects with the lunar nodes, Sun and Mars. These shorter transits to a slow moving planet creates heighten energy that produces news events. Saturn in Scorpio is already working in the background but the news reports will happen with the addition of the shorter transits.

Many writers in American astrology magazines have been predicting the Great Cardinal Climax of 2008-2016 with a series of hard aspects between Saturn, Uranus and Pluto from 2008 to 2015. The financial crisis of 2008 came with the first of these aspects occurred with Saturn opposing Uranus in the cardinal signs of Libra and Aries. Then in 2010, Uranus started an interlocking dance with Pluto going in and out of a squaring aspect six times until 2015. The Arab Spring of 2011 didn't just happen. Uranus was moving out of Pisces into Aries to form a long square to Pluto in Capricorn (2011-2015). Saturn was in Libra (laws and government seeking equality/fairness). So there was a wide t-square in the sky of Saturn, Uranus and Pluto. In early January 2011 we had a solar eclipse at 13 Capricorn that set things off with Saturn at 16 Libra and Mars was involved with this eclipse in early Capricorn. Frustration was high when Tunisia exploded. It took Mars to enter Aquarius in mid-January 2011 to light the fuse all over the Arab countries of Egypt, Libya, Yemen, Syria and Bahrain. When the Sun also entered Aquarius (sign of revolution) in January, the Egyptian youth overthrew Mubarak in late January 2011. There were worldwide protests, not just in the Middle East. It grew to a peak when the planets of the Sun, Venus, Mars, Jupiter and Uranus were in Aries, and Saturn opposed this cluster while Pluto squared it all in Capricorn. Youth were rebelling around the world and they were militant. It generated the Occupy Wall Street Movement in October 2011 that spread around the world. This long five-year square of Uranus in Aries (change, revolution, rebellion with military action by youth) creates frustration and stubborn resistance (the square) to maintain the status quo of corporate interests and government with military force (Pluto in Capricorn) with the use of stalemate and non-action. It takes the eclipses and fast moving planets like the Sun and Mars to reach multiple crisis points.

The first quarter of 2011 was a very special time period because there was excess volatility in the sky. The suicide in Tunisia happen in mid-January but it wasn't until Mars had entered Aquarius (a combination of violence) and then the Sun had entered Aquarius (a sign of revolution) that Egypt erupted too. Next, Jupiter entered Aries to join up with Pluto (social change by the young). Another element was added too with Jupiter and Pluto squaring the lunar nodes (more surprises and changes to the establishment).[18]

The March-April 2011 was a very special period. In mid-March there was a Moon Wobble (Sun square the lunar nodes) with Uranus squaring these points the week of the Japanese tsunami. By early April there was a major cluster of planets in Aries (Sun, Venus, Mars, Jupiter and Uranus) with Saturn and Pluto in aspect to the cluster. Here is a list of events:

Mar 11th - An earthquake measuring 9.0 in magnitude struck 130 km (80 miles) east of Sendai, Japan, which triggered a tsunami that killed thousands of people. This event also triggered the second largest nuclear accident in history, and one of only two events to be classified as a Level 7 on the International Nuclear Event Scale.

Mar 12th - A reactor at the Fukushima Daiichi Nuclear Power Plant melts and exploded and released radioactivity into the atmosphere a day after Japan's earthquake.

Apr 1st - After protests against the burning of the Quran turned violent, a mob attacked a United Nations compound in Mazar-i-Sharif, Afghanistan and killed thirteen people, including eight foreign workers.

Apr 9th - A gunman murdered five people, injured eleven, and committed suicide in a mall in the Netherlands.

Apr 11th - Minsk Metro bombing

Apr 19th - Fidel Castro resigned from the Communist Party of Cuba's central committee after 45 years of holding the title.

Apr 25th - At least 300 people killed in deadliest tornado outbreak in the Southern United States since the 1974 Super Outbreak.

Apr 27th - The deadliest day of the 2011 Super outbreak of tornadoes, the largest tornado outbreak, in United States history.

Apr 27th - U.S. President Barack Obama, coerced by incessant false "birther" accusations, publicly released a copy of his birth certificate.[19]

Here is the chart for this time period with a cluster of planets in Aries and a conjunction of Mars and Uranus squaring the lunar nodes. This is a period of abrupt violent change and upheaval. This chart is not for a specific event but is representative of this time period. The houses are not important but the signs and aspects are. There are five planets in Aries, a sign noted for extreme intensity, obsession and massive events. The conjunction of Mars and Uranus, which is a violent combination, was in Aries. Adding the lunar nodes in square to this aspect just added more dynamite. Both of these planets were in exact declination to each other. Having the same declination can add intensity to an aspect. In addition, the Sun is opposing Saturn to add frustrations and limitations to the mix. The events listed above reflect these aspects.

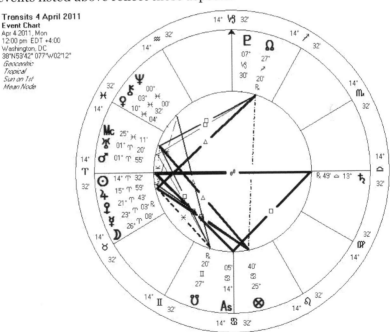

Transits for April 4, 2011

Below is the chart for the first Nuclear Explosion at Fukushima. Note that the planet Uranus (associated with shocking events) had just entered Aries, ruled by Pluto. Pluto is associated with radiation, nuclear matters and massive disasters like plagues or mass murders like war. Pluto at 7 Capricorn was in a wide t-square with Saturn at 15 Libra and Jupiter at 10 Aries. The lunar nodes were in aspect to Uranus so it increased the volatile factor of this event. There was a hidden element with Mars at 13Pi35. It was squaring the node of Uranus at 14Geo2. This position on the heliocentric node of Uranus created a Mars square Uranus aspect, not seen in the chart. There was a second explosion on March 14th and a third on March 15th as transiting Mars moved off the node of Uranus by one degree, so it was still in aspect to the node of Uranus. The Fukushima disaster has not finished being played out in 2014. They were still removing spent fuel rods out of the reactors in 2014 and there was a massive amount of radioactive water stored on site that was leaking into the ground water. This was a class 7 event that will mark the world for years to come. The seriousness of this disaster is not over yet

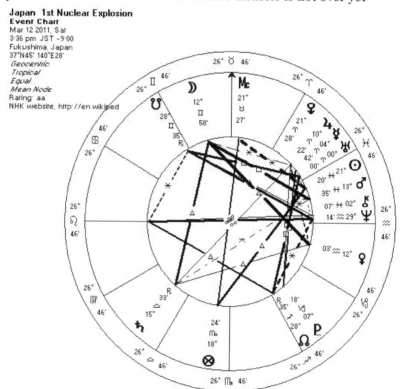

Japan 1st Nuclear Explosion
Event Chart
Mar 12 2011, Sat
3:36 pm JST -9:00
Fukushima, Japan
37°N45' 140°E28'
Geocentric
Tropical
Equal
Mean Node
Rating: aa
NHK website, http://en.wikiped

Fukushima Nuclear Explosion

As this is written in the summer of 2014, the world is still in the middle of these events that are still unfolding with Pluto square Uranus. In August 2014 there was an unjust killing of a black teenager in Ferguson, Missouri. The police went into riot control mode and brought out all the military gear they had been purchasing from Home Land Security. It caused a major backlash from the public and was nicknamed Fergustan because our police force has become militarized in their behavior, treating citizens like they are the enemy.[20]

Solar Arabic Parts

The Solar Arabic Parts or Greek Lots I find very useful, but only if there is a correctly timed chart with the time of day given. These are some of the oldest techniques back to the Hellenistic Greeks in Egypt but the Persians greatly expanded the use of the Parts and added many, many more. The Solar Parts are unique among Arabic Parts since they are measuring the distance the Sun has travel from the Ascendant. The Hellenistic Egyptians were obsessed with the horizon. They measured the Sun rising and setting. They believed that the Goddess Nut swallowed the Sun at sunset and it coursed through her body at night. At sunrise she expelled the sun as if she was giving birth to the renewed Sun rising on the horizon. The relationship of the horizon to the Sun was a constant measurement of the night and day hours. Every major holiday and season was measured from the Sun.

This is a form of duality between the movement of the sky against the stationary houses. It is fundamental to the relationship of the movement of the signs in the daily motion of the Earth against the houses that are stationary measurements at the natal position.

If one is standing on Earth, the sun will appear to rise at sunrise and move across the sky to set in the west. The sky appears to move around us but in reality, it is the Earth that is rotating daily on its own axis. This makes the sky move daily.

If the Arabic Parts are looked at as a form of fractal geometry, then the Egyptians were measuring the inverse ratio of the horizon to the Sun with the Solar Parts.

The traditional formula we see in astrology books and software is:

Part of Fortune	= Ascendant + Moon	– Sun
Part of Commerce	= Ascendant + Mercury	– Sun
Part of Love	= Ascendant + Venus	– Sun
Part of Passion	= Ascendant + Mars	– Sun
Part of Increase	= Ascendant + Jupiter	– Sun
Part of Fatality	= Ascendant + Saturn	– Sun
Part of Catastrophe	= Ascendant + Uranus	– Sun
Part of Treachery	= Ascendant + Neptune	– Sun
Part of Organization	= Ascendant + Pluto	– Sun

The important ratio that is being measured is Ascendant – Sun. Let's go back to the first explosion of Fukushima as a working example for Solar Parts.

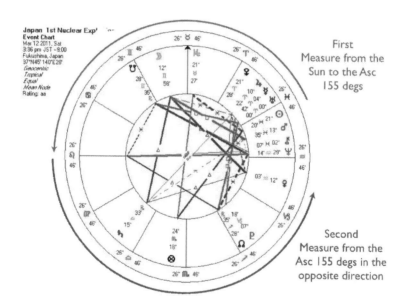

Visual Measurement of Arabic Parts for Fukushima

Natal, Planets maintain their house positions.

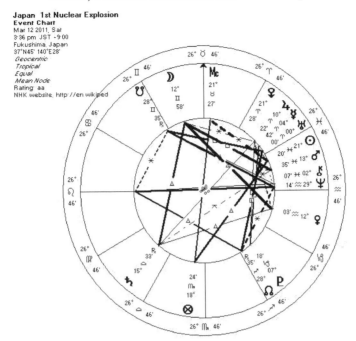

Solar Parts Chart, the Part of the Sun equal Natal Asc

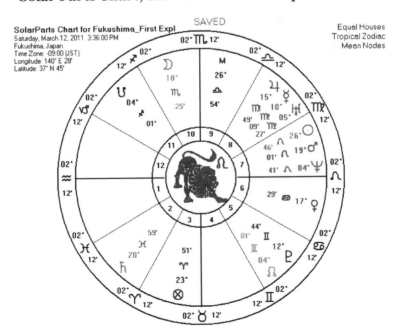

This measurement of the distance of the Sun from the Ascendant creates a mirrored effect, like looking at a reflection. The Solar Parts chart[21] moves one degree every two minutes. A natal chart moves one degree every four minutes. This is like a shadow effect of the Sun to the Ascendant. It's fractal geometry applied to astrology and astronomy. It is a lot like a snowflake that has six sides and that are duplicated on the opposite side into 12 arms. In the Solar Parts chart, the planets have maintained their house positions exactly. The Part of Sun is exactly the same as the Natal Ascendant position. I have re-named the Solar Parts by their planetary names so that I'm not prejudiced by the loaded words like Fatality, Catastrophe or Treachery and it clarifies which planet the Part represents.

Part of Moon	18Sc25
Part of Mercury	10Vi09
Part of Venus	17Ca29
Part of Mars	19Le01
Part of Jupiter	15Vi49
Part of Saturn	20Pi59
Part of Uranus	05Vi27
Part of Neptune	04Le41
Part of Pluto	12Ge44
Part of Sun	26Le46
Part of Self	02Le12

Carl Payne Tobey had studied these Arabic Parts for years. He was always looking for the hidden geometry behind the astrology, the mathematical patterns. He had a strong transiting Venus and Jupiter crossing his chart for one week in 1957. He got a eureka moment, he saw the pattern, so he rushed back to his house to draw up his own chart with the Solar Parts. He had discovered a new Part that fit the old pattern of Ascendant + Planet – Sun. The new part was 8 degrees of Leo. The sign Leo hit home with Tobey. For decades, astrologers had guessed his sign as Leo, not Sun in Taurus or Sagittarius rising. He didn't have anything important in Leo. This new part was the Part of Self, a new secondary Ascendant. With this one point he could draw a Solar Parts chart. The mathematical pattern was complete and the hidden design was revealed.

Let's look at the declinations of Fukushima before I analyze it more:

Japan 1st Nuclear Explosion		Fukushima, Japan
Event Chart		37°N45' 140°E28'
Mar 12 2011, Sat	Equal	Geocentric, Tropical
3:36 pm JST -9:00		Mean Node

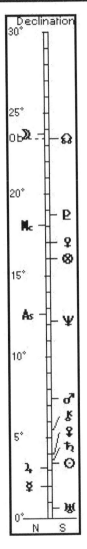

Pt	Decl.	Long.	L.E.Dec
♅	-00°38'	00°♈00	28°♓23
☿	+01°58'	04°♈42	04°♈58
♃	+03°05'	10°♈22	07°♈48
☉	-03°26'	21°♓20	21°♓20
♄	-03°38'	15°♎33	09°♎10
♀	-04°00'	21°♈28	19°♓52
⚷	-05°28'	02°♓07	16°♓06
♂	-07°23'	13°♓35	11°♓06
♆	-12°11'	29°♒14	27°♒54
As	+12°35'	26°♌46	26°♌46
⊗	-16°00'	18°♏24	13°♏52
♀	-17°00'	12°♒03	12°♒40
Mc	+18°07'	21°♉27	21°♉27
♇	-18°45'	07°♑18	06°♒04
☋	+23°25'	28°♊35	28°♊35
☊	-23°25'	28°♐35	28°♐35
☽	+23°42'	12°♊58	21°♊36

Declinations for Fukushima

The natal Moon is Out of Bounds (OOB). Saturn and the Sun are in parallel declination to each other. The rest of the declination points are not very important. What about the Solar Parts? I only use the Solar Parts that add information to the Natal chart. The Part of Saturn is conjunct the natal Sun and we know that Mars and Saturn are in the same declination. This adds a double emphasis on Saturn and the Sun but there is also a square aspect to the lunar nodes (they are high declination too) that is forming a t-square to the Sun. Traditional astrology call this a Lunar Bending, Tobey called it a Moon Wobble. It creates instability like a solar eclipse without a shadow blocking the Sun. So this is a period of chaotic instability that is forming into exactness in five days. Natal Uranus is already in a close square to the Lunar Nodes. This points to major surprises and explosions, or shocking events to unfold as the Sun approaches Uranus and exactly squares the Lunar Nodes.

Because of the 3:36 pm time, I look at the Solar Arabic Parts for more information, for more hidden meaning. The Part of Pluto is conjunct the natal Moon that is OOB and this Part of Pluto is also square natal Mars. This Part of Pluto has pulled in a wild erratic OOB Moon that is already being squared by natal Mars. This is a very important Part since Pluto is strongly associated with radiation and massive plagues. Could this help point to a slow evolving increase of cancer diseases because of increased levels of radiation in our foods around the world? The chart points to instability and ongoing surprises. The next two days, more reactors overheated and exploded. The natal Saturn quincunx Mars indicates hiding the truth about long-term health issues. The Diichi management of the Fukushima Power plant lied to the government and to the world about the seriousness of this disaster. The US government was so concerned, it sent out its own scientists to Fukushima to independently evaluate the situation. It was a crisis of the highest magnitude. A few Diichi employees and firemen risked their lives trying to get the meltdown under control to save Japan and the world. Neptune was on the natal Descendant that indicates hidden forces and the ocean. It could represent hiding the truth from the public or preventing full public disclosure. This saga is not resolved yet. More will unfold in the near future by 2016.

In April 2014, there was a rare Grand Cardinal Square of Pluto, Uranus, Jupiter and Mars. It occurred with a lunar and solar eclipse during the same month. Vladimir Putin had invaded Crimea in late February and early March 2014. As this aspect formed in April, he invaded Ukraine with Russian troops disguised as pro-Russian Ukrainians. That put Russia in conflict with Germany and the USA.

It got pretty heated but the Russians stayed in place without much movement until transiting Mars, that had been retrograde, turned direct in May. Then the Ukrainian government sent out troops to fight back against the Russians. In June Putin cut off gas supplies to Ukraine and the US imposed sanctions against seven Russian businessmen. The conflict is ongoing with a stalemate that is not resolved at this point.[22]   On the following page is the graphic timeline for Putin.

I expected more events to develop in April 2014 but they didn't happen or they didn't make the news. But many times there are delays in the reporting of major changes that are brewing beneath the surface. This came true with the invasion of ISIS taking control of a major part of Iraq in early June 2014 by al-Baghdadi, who was born in 1971. The rally cry of ISIS/ISIL is that they want to un-do the Sykes-Picot Agreement of 1916 that forced the division of the Arab counties for the benefit of the English and French after WW I, ignoring the tribal differences that existed at that time and now. ISIS/ISIL has been fighting in Syria and in June 2014; they turned their eye on Iraq to consolidate the Sunni peoples.   It was a bold power grab, very similar to Putin with Ukraine.

Note the transit of Mars during this time period when it retrograded in April (ISIS planned their military moves). Then, when it turned direct ISIS started their military actions to invade Iraq and extend their influence. The transit of Saturn against the Sykes-Picot Agreement chart on Uranus was a clear indication that ISIS will play the long game to breakup this agreement. It's doubly reflected a second time with the Grand Cross and transiting Mars on the Skyes-Picot. They are determined to break the status quo by force. I would use al-Baghdadi's chart but we only know his year 1971. When transiting Jupiter and the lunar node crossed against the Skyes-Picot chart in mid-July 2014, there was more foreign intervention by the USA by adding 800 troops to Bagdad and additional funds given from Saudi Arabia to ISIS. As of August 7th, the USA started to bomb ISIS in Iraq as this is written.

We cannot use the Solar Parts since this agreement does not have a time of day. But the declinations can be examined.

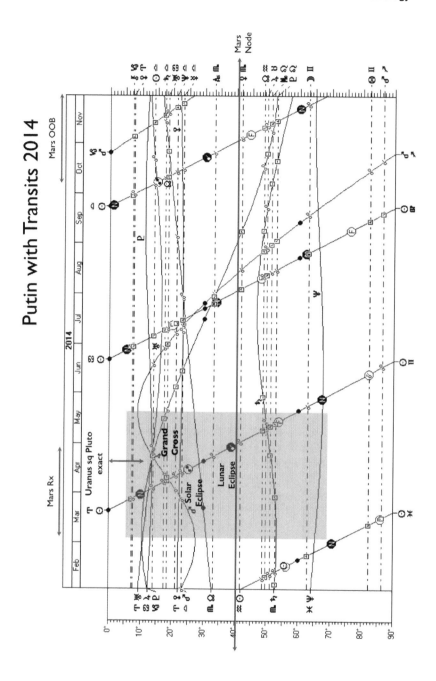

Timeline Graph of Transits with Putin's Natal Chart

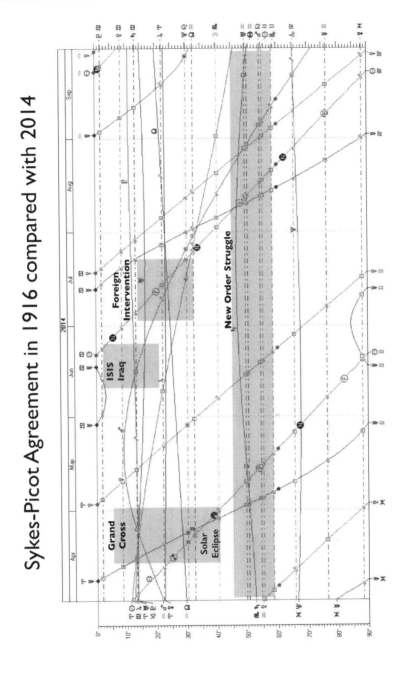

Sykes-Picot Agreement in 1916 compared with 2014

Sykes-Picot 1916 Natal with 2014 Hard Aspects

Sykes-Picot Agreement		Paris, France
Natal Chart		48°N52' 002°E20'
May 16 1916, Tue	Equal	Geocentric, Tropical
12:00 pm UT +0:00		Mean Node

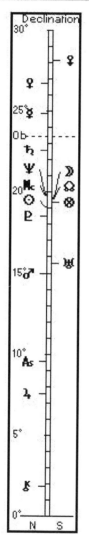

Pt	Decl.	Long.	L.E.Dec
☊	+01°50'	25°♓31	04°♈36
♃	+07°33'	22°♈03	19°♈18
As	+09°31'	05°♍26	05°♍26
♂	+14°57'	24°♌28	19°♌33
♅	-15°34'	19°♒40	17°♒32
♇	+18°31'	01°♋54	07°♌01
☉	+19°05'	25°♉15	25°♉15
⊗	-19°22'	20°♒31	03°♒30
☊	-19°36'	02°♒31	02°♒31
☋	+19°36'	02°♌31	02°♌31
☽	-19°39'	10°♏20	27°♏43
Mc	+19°49'	28°♉26	28°♉26
♆	+19°50'	00°♌13	01°♌26
♄	+22°35'	13°♋12	15°♋07
☿	+24°51'	16°♊20	10°♊41
♀	+26°43'	08°♋32	29°♋32
♀	-28°10'	28°♓07	05°♒32

Sykes-Picot 1916 Declinations

Venus and Mercury were Out of Bounds (OOB) and Saturn was in high declination. The Agreement was formed under a Mars opposition Uranus in fixed signs that adds longevity to the Agreement and they were both near the same declination, this adds more power to the aspect. Note that the heliocentric node of Mars was at 19Ta06 and square Uranus at 19Aq40. Wikipedia didn't state why this Agreement was made quickly. More than likely, it was created under a panic and a high sense of urgency.With the OOB Venus, OOB Mercury and Hydek Saturn; no consideration was made to the peoples involved in the writing of this legal agreement and it was hastily drawn. Amazingly, the British also preplanned for a Zion state with this Agreement in 1916 and the Balfour Agreement of 1917.

As this is written, Israel has been attacking the Giza strip to push back at Hamas when Mars entered Scorpio. The whole area is in turmoil and al Baghdadi has sworn to undo this Agreement. With the long term Uranus square Pluto in place, it will be done with much chaos and destruction as these aspects un-balance the Middle East and pits Saudi Arabia against Iran. It will be interesting to follow the transits as each event unfolds in the near future.

Dispositorship and Reception

When a planet is in it's own sign, it is a final depositor of itself, such as Sun in Leo or Jupiter in Sagittarius. But if a planet is in a sign it does not rule, then the ruler of the sign influences it. Dispositorship is a form of modification of influence for a planet's placement in a sign. For example, if Mars is in Sagittarius, Jupiter in Sagittarius is the depositor of Mars. This can become a very long chain of depositors if most planets are not in their own sign. My experience is that one level of dispositorship is enough in most analysis. If the wrong planetary rulers are used in the first place, then the dispositorship is questionable. If Jupiter is in Aries, the proper depositor is Pluto, not Mars (the traditional co-ruler.) This becomes complicated when dealing with Uranus as the ruler of Aquarius, Neptune as the ruler of Pisces or Pluto as the ruler of Aries. The three discovered planets affect the Dignities and Dispositorship, so the newly discovered planets are ignored by Traditionalists. If Uranus is on the ascendant in Pisces, it seems grossly wrong to look to what sign Jupiter is in. I would look to Neptune. Mutual reception means that two planets are in each other's signs, like Venus in Sagittarius and Jupiter in Libra. Reception compliments the planets mutually. The planets can create compatibility. Where this concept is in doubt is if Saturn is in Pisces and Neptune is in Capricorn. These two signs and their rulers are not complimentary.

Decans

Two very old techniques that have survived until modern times is a reflection of fractal geometry applied to astrology. It is the concept of first dividing the circle of the ecliptic into the twelve signs, then each sign can be divided again by three to make 36 divisions called the Decans. This division of the sky goes back to the Egyptians that had a 360 day year plus five holidays to adjust the solar calendar. They used a 10 day week that measured the night hours by a star on the horizon. Each measuring star could be used for 10 days until another one was used to mark the night hours. However, the texts and techniques that used the Decans are confusing with multiple ways to use them. These Decans still need to be sorted out and analyzed with large amounts of data to figure out what works.

The other division is to divide the twelve signs by twelve again, making 144 divisions. For me, I find that this technique is too fine a division for me to discern any differences between 2.5 degrees within a sign. However, I know that the Jyotish astrologers continue to use these divisions and many other divisions in the dasa systems. I mention this for further study and examination. The principles are sound but more analysis and observations need to be done by future researchers to find if there is value in these 144 divisions. Below is how these divisions are made:

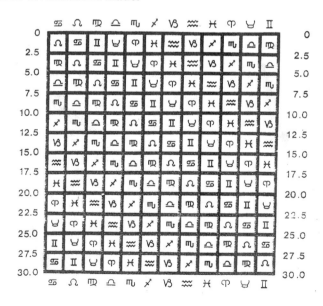

The 2.5 degree Division of the Zodiac

I have ordered the best techniques by importance and transits are the most reliable for predictive use. The intent of this chapter is for others struggling with reliability in forecasting to use these recommendations above other techniques. Hopefully with testing of these techniques, clarity and accuracy will improve others personal experience. Believe in your own ability to test astrology's principles in your own life and see it reflected in events around you.

In general, to do more accurate predictions, it is necessary to know the twelve astrological principles well as signs, planets and houses; but also the subject that is being studied. Most financial astrologers have a background in the financial industry. It helps to have medical training to do medical astrology. To be knowledgeable in seismology is helpful for predicting earthquakes.

Footnotes

1. http://en.wikipedia.org/wiki/Ptolemy
   Ptolemy presented a useful tool for astronomical calculations in his *Handy Tables*, which tabulated all the data needed to compute the positions of the Sun, Moon and planets, the rising and setting of the stars, and eclipses of the Sun and Moon. Ptolemy's Handy Tables provided the model for later astronomical tables or zījes. In the *Phaseis (Risings of the Fixed Stars)*, Ptolemy gave a *parapegma*, a star calendar or almanac, based on the hands and disappearances of stars over the course of the solar year...
   Because Ptolemy derived many of his key latitudes from crude longest day values, his latitudes are erroneous on average by roughly a degree (2 degrees for Byzantium, 4 degrees for Carthage), though capable ancient astronomers knew their latitudes to more like a minute. (Ptolemy's own latitude was in error by 14'.) He agreed that longitude was best determined by simultaneous observation of lunar eclipses, yet he was so out of touch with the scientists of his day that he knew of no such data more recent than 500 years before (Arbela eclipse).
2. http://en.wikipedia.org/wiki/Astrolabe
   An early astrolabe was invented in the Hellenistic world in 150 BC and is often attributed to Hipparchus. A marriage of the planisphere and, the astrolabe was effectively an analog calculator capable of working out several different kinds of problems in spherical astronomy. Theon of Alexandria wrote a detailed treatise on the astrolabe, and Lewis (2001) argues that Ptolemy used an astrolabe to make the astronomical observations recorded in the *Tetrabilblos*.
3. http://en.wikipedia.org/wiki/Kepler%27s_laws_of_planetary_motion

Johannes Kepler published his first two laws about planetary motion in 1609, having found them by analyzing the astronomical observations of Tycho Brahe. Kepler's third law was published in 1619...Kepler in 1621 and Godefroy Wendelin in 1643 noted that Kepler's third law applies to the four brightest moons of Jupiter. The second law ("area law" form) was contested by Nicolaus Mercator in a book from 1664; but by 1670 he was publishing in its favour in *Philosophical Transactions*, and as the century proceeded it became more widely accepted. The reception in Germany changed noticeably between 1688, the year in which Newton's Principia was published and was taken to be basically Copernican, and 1690, by which time work of Gottried Leibniz on Kepler had been published.

4. http://ephemeris.com/history/modern-theories.html

On the fateful night of 7 January 1610, Galileo trained a new 30 power telescope on Jupiter and discovered three of the four easily visible moons of Jupiter.... He reasoned that the motion of these moons around Jupiter proved that not everything revolved around the Earth...Galileo also discovered the rings of Saturn, but died not knowing that they were rings. ...Galileo supported the theory of Copernicus, that planets and the Earth revolved around the Sun... Another astronomer familiar with Copernicus' *De revolutionibus orbium coelestium*, Tycho Brahe, Imperial mathematician in Prague in the late 1500s, made painstaking observations of the Sun, Moon, and planets throughout much of his life. ...Tycho Brahe did not support the new heliocentric theory of Copernicus...Driven by a desire to solve the mystery of planetary orbits, he constructed the most accurate observatory that existed before the telescope's invention. His data was the most accurate that had ever been recorded at the time. He published a paper in 1573, *De nova stella*, that described a supernova observation. This observation refuted the common belief that the heavens were fixed, never changing. His careful observations of the Moon allowed him to determine formulas for lunar motion with unprecedented accuracy...he began work on a theory that would explain his decades of careful planetary observations. He had already found that the Earth did not remain a constant distance to the Sun throughout a year, in 1591. However, he was not able to explain or further investigate this phenomenon before his death on October 24, 1601... As he was dying, Tycho Brahe said to his assistant, Johannes Kepler, "Do not let me have lived in vain." While Kepler showed that Brahe's geocentric beliefs were not true, it was only by using his highly accurate data spanning decades that Kepler was able to develop his own theories of planetary motion. In that sense, Tycho Brahe had not endeavored all those years in vain, for he laid the groundwork necessary for Kepler's amazing mathematical discoveries.

The greatest astronomical records in the world were those of Tycho Brahe. At the same time, Brahe needed someone with Kepler's mathematical abilities to analyze his extensive data. Kepler joined him as an assistant in February 1600, the year before Tycho Brahe's death. Kepler believed in the Copernican system, which placed the Sun at the center of the Solar System. He had begun investigating the motion of Mars before Tycho Brahe's death. Kepler's understanding of planetary motion accelerated when he realized that the orbit of Mars was in a plane tilted slightly from the plane of the Earth's orbit around the Sun. He published his observations on Mars in 1609. Why was predicting the orbit of Mars such a great achievement? It was because no other planet exhibits as severe retrograde (backwards) motion as Mars when viewed from the Earth. Mercury and Venus always stay close to the Sun. Jupiter and Saturn, the other known planets at the time, are further away. Mars is the closest planet to the Earth that is farther from the Sun than the Earth, and so its retrograde motion appears the greatest. **There was no other planetary orbit that was more difficult to predict than the orbit of Mars**. Kepler then sought to discover general rules that explained the motions of all the planets. After trying numerous theories, Kepler discovered three incredible laws of planetary motion. Today these are often referred to as K1, K2, and K3:

K1: The planets orbit the sun in an elliptical orbit, with the Sun at one of the focus points of the ellipse.

K2: The planets sweep across an equal area between themselves and the Sun in an equal amount of time.

K3: The squares of the periods of two planets orbiting the Sun are proportional to the cubes of their semi-major axes (half of the long axis of their orbital ellipse).

Kepler proposed that planetary motion was caused by magnetic force from the Sun. **Astronomers calculated reference ephemerides by using elliptical orbits for almost 400 years after Kepler's discovery. It wasn't until the 1970s** that computer technology and NASA's need to accurately send spacecraft to planets that more accurate computer simulations of mutual gravitational attraction of Solar System bodies became practical. To this day, positions of asteroids of unknown mass are still calculated using Kepler's elliptical orbits. Later in the 1600s, Sir Isaac Newton formulated the principles of gravitational attraction. Newton's breakthrough came from contemplating Kepler's Third Law. He said that he first found in 1680 that the pattern of a planet under gravitational attraction from the Sun would be an ellipse with the Sun at one focus. Unfortunately, he lost the proof in his office. At the urging of his friend, astronomer Edmond Halley (of Halley's Comet fame), in 1684 Newton spent three months reconstructing the proof.

5. Holden, James Herschel, *A History of Horoscopic Astrology*, A.F.A., Inc., 2006, p. 148

Ptolemy had Planetary Tables but they were very inaccurate by 700 years the time of Albumasar's time. So the Arabs began to review the accuracy of their tables every generation or so... Things did not improve until Kepler published his Rudolphine Tables in 1627

6. *Raphael's Astronomical Ephemeris of the Planets' Places for 1901*, W Foulsham & Co., Ltd, London, UK., back page.

"The most difficult and least understood part of Astrology is the *Directional*, or the calculation of future events. There are Zodiacal directions, Mundane directions, Secondary directions, Secondary directions, progressed cusps, Revolutional figures, Eclipses, New Moons, etc., etc., until in short, if they are all calculated in detail, there would be at least, an important influence every week on an average. The stern facts of life do not bear out such copious influences, and it is practically a waste of time to work out the Primaries, as they are called, when not more than 10 per cent will be found to coincide with an event. I regret I must adhere to the opinion so often expressed, which, that none of our systems of Directions are correct, but that the Secondary as taught in my "Key" comes nearer to the truth than any, yet it is sadly deficient and unreliable. I do not take the planets as symbols, but as forces, producing, or causing the events that occur during our pilgrimage on this earth. The True Key to Astrology was lost centuries ago, and has not yet been found.

Our knowledge of the Zodiac is sadly deficient, and it is this deficiency that causes so many failures; there is no doubt that some degrees are very unfortunate or malignant and others the reverse, whereas in our present state of knowledge all the degrees are alike in nature, yet we know from observation that there are not two things exactly alike in creation. What causes the difference except it be the Zodiac?"

7. Bennett, Sydney K., *The Key Cycle by Wynn*, American Federation of Astrologers 1970, p.2-6.

"There are several ways the planets effect this excitation, or stimulation, chief among which are:
Primary Directions
Progressions or secondary directions
Transits through the natal horoscope
Combinations of any two or all three of the foregoing
The Key Cycle [a modified form of Solar Returns]

More than a score (20) of years studying all the methods of predictions I could find in the first four classifications led me to the discovery of the Key cycle. This was because none of the other four methods was satisfactory; none of them could stand up over a period years, nor could any of them account for all the actual influences one does meet with in life. And not one of these four stands the test of reason. The Key Cycle is the result of reasoning out factors of astronomy and bring one dominant but hitherto unused factor unto the field of astrological applications....

Primary directions, usually referred as to 'directions,' are not rational for they are based on the notion that all the influences of a man's life occur while he is yet in the cradle, that the conditions of a life on ninety years are completely shown by the rotation of the earth in the native's first six hours.

The same irrationality is attached to 'progressions,' except that the time element is slightly longer-- a complete lifetime of say, ninety years being theoretically epitomized in the native's first 90 days, while he is still in the cradle. This is the day-for-a-year method. Says Alfred Pearce in The Textbook of Astrology of 1911, "I have never found any progressions effective in my own nativity."

And then he dismisses the entire method with a single paragraph. He states previously in the same work that progressions arose from an added idea of Placidus, the Spanish monk who translated Ptolemy in 1647 and 1757. The idea was introduced by this translator in his work Primum Mobile. "Prior to 1816," continues Pearce, "the various translations of Ptolemy and Placidus were wretched and misleading and led to many errors on the parts of Lilly, Colley, Sibley, Gadbury and others when they treated on the method of timing life's influences. They mixed the erroneous system of horary divinations with the science of natal astrology. It is lamentable to find that this folly is still taught and practiced even to the present day."

...Most students are modest. They are unwilling to believe themselves as good thinkers as those who have written books, which is often a mistake; most books are rehashed mistranslations of the real thought someone once had. If you really can think for yourself, do so; come to your own conclusions.

This unwillingness of students to challenge the statements of authors has made much trouble. The student, realizing many of his actual shortcomings, often believes himself poorer than he really is and believes he will someday see the logic of directions and progressions, or that he has not quite obtained the proper method for figuring them or interpreting them.

Permit me to state without qualification that I have gone through these stages. I have doubted my own doubts, and I have vindicated them. I can figure directions and progressions and have done so in many thousands of cases. I have believed in them to the extent of backing them with hard-earned money. I have lost heavily by so doing. For directions and progressions are nonexistent. There is no such actual thing or influence as either of them and the sooner astrologers discard them as a fantasy of the ignorant Middle Ages the sooner will astrologers be able to avoid the many false hopes and groundless warnings they produce for themselves and others...

The foregoing and many other considerations had been in my mind for years when in 1926, I had an accident for which I could find no suggestion in any of the methods I had been able to find in the book I had...

That accident was nearly fatal. It occurred in May 18, 1926 at approximately 9:00 pm., at Merced, California. I was injured on the head and hip; stuck by a hit-and-run auto. I was on a business trip at the time; after several previous losing attempts I was seeking again to take advantage of what I considered a most marvelous combination of progressions; progressed Moon trine natal Sun and progressed Sun trine natal Moon...I was then in desperate business and financials circumstances. The trip was a complete failure in a commercial way...

My first reaction was distinctly against astrology and included great resentment against the books that had caused me to waste, as I thought then, more than 10 precious years of my life. And I thought of the times clients had reported failure of progressions and directions and how I had replied that they were doubtless misinformed as to their birth times. I even had the idea of turning my abilities against astrology, planning to write up the failures of progressions and directions. I went over the texts and their examples and attacked them without the customary attitude of the astrological student--without hoping they would work. And I saw much. I saw supposedly reputable writers stretching and distorting and making things look more accurate and scientific than they were. These analyses of well-known texts were written up in part in the January and February 1932 issues of the AFA Bulletin under the titles "Mis-Directions" and "Progress vs. Progressions."

8.   Lewi, Grant, *Heaven Knows What*, Llewellyn Publications 1969, p. 9.
      "Grant Lewi did not use progressions. He did not use fixed stars. He found everything he wanted in the solar system. He was a practical rather than a theoretical astrologer. He wasn't concerned with why astrology works. He was more concerned with the fact that it does. This was no more unexpected or mysterious to him than the fact that trees grow. We don't know how or why. He was more concerned with astrology as the only real key to psychological understanding of self than

with any of its other phases."

9. Tobey, Carl Payne, Correspondence Course, Lesson 18, 1957.

"We cannot ignore the fact that there have been many students who have adopted progressions because they claimed to have found they work, while there have been many other students who discarded progressions because they claimed to have found they did not work. Thus, we have confusion. The witnesses do not testify to the same thing. What witnesses are we to believe?

Throughout these 27 years, while the writer has been known as a transitist, it might be noted that he has never published an actual opinion relative to progressions. He has never said YES and he has never said NO, but there comes a time when one must speak, and in putting out this Course on astrology, it becomes impossible to ignore the matter of progressions. Actually, we have seen progressions work and we have seen them fail to work. In essence, what we should say is that they have not worked accurately.

In 1926, when first studying astrology in the form of the work of Llewellyn George, we looked ahead, and we read up what was supposed to happen to us a long time hence. According to George, the writer might become the father of a child after he was 40, when progressed Venus reached his natal Sun. At the time of making this study the writer was 24 and a child had been born in that year. It is interesting to note that he had no more children until after he was 41, when his only son was born. However, the birth was off by several years. That is typical of the writer's experience with progressions. He found that they worked but they did not work at the right time. There were broad inaccuracies. In some cases, they worked very accurately, but in most instances, they did not. It is not the writer's nature to impulsively toss this sort of evidence out the window and merely say that progressions do not work. There is nothing unusual about this kind of evidence...

The writer never used progressions in advising clients during all of the years of his professional practice, because he found that he could not depend on their accuracy although he could depend on the accuracy of transits. Nevertheless, he has always kept an open mind. Where there is smoke, there might be fire. We will later discuss what might be wrong with progressions and how they might possibly be found to work with accuracy. First, however, let us take up the claim of some that progressions are ridiculous. How could the planets on the 23rd day after your birth have anything to do with the 23rd year of your life? This question is based on the assumption that astrology is a causal phenomenon. We have held that it is not, and when you stop assuming that it is, new avenues open up to you. There is the possibility that progressions might involve some form of mathematical expression, and abstract cosmic design whereby there is a relationship between rotations and revolutions of the earth. We do not know. It is merely a possibility. If progressions work inaccurately, we should not toss them out. We should investigate more thoroughly. We should try and find out why. The first automobiles did not run very efficiently, but we did not throw out the whole idea, although there were many people who advised doing so. Progressions in the right hands might turn up something we do not yet know.

One of the great difficulties with many progressionists is that they are fatalistic in their attitude and they work with an expected precision that does not exist. They try to calculate an aspect such as one of Mars-Saturn down to an exact day when accuracy does not even appear to be to an exact year. Some progressed aspects would be of very long duration, and would not apply for a specific event to occur on a certain day. When the writer was a child, progressed Mars moved over his natal Sun, and that interval was certainly accompanied by a couple of years when he was always getting hurt through falls, etc. There was no other similar period in his life. The opposition of progressed Mercury to Uranus in his chart coincided with his editorship of the Long Beach (N.Y.) Sun, as a youngster, which resulted in a spectacular editorial campaign against political corruption in Nassau County, which in turn lead to a state investigation being ordered by Governor Alfred E. Smith, and this ultimately led to conviction of many public officials and the end of a political regime. You will realize that many enemies resulted. Immediately thereafter, Mercury crossed the writer's 7th natal cusp, and he was married for the first time, while visiting in Palm Beach. When progressed Mercury reached the conjunction of Neptune in his chart, he began writing for astrology magazines. During the years when progressed Mars was squaring his Jupiter, he went through a period of terrific gambling losses. In fact, almost anything he did business wise lost money, but fortunately he was very young. He was coming out of his teens. Things were more than tough when the progressed ascendant reached natal Saturn. When the progressed ascendant reached natal Jupiter, he moved from New York to Arizona and began a new era.

On the other hand, many of the most important events of his life were accompanied by no significant progressions. Now and then, however, we have a case that baffles us, and we turn to progressions to see what they might show. Here is a lady who is seized with pain in the middle of the night, is rushed to a hospital and goes through an emergency appendectomy. Mars was exactly on her natal Sun and Pluto, but it had crossed that point once every two years of her life with no operation necessary and without any similar ailments. Why did it happen this time? We turn to progressions, and we find that her progressed Mars has reached her natal Sun, so that the transit of Mars was over a progressed Mars conjunct her Sun-Pluto in Cancer. Such cases might be coincidence, but are they?

It has been our experience that transits work to natal cusps of houses computed in the plane of the earth's orbit and not to the cusps of houses computed in accord with the Placidian system. The progressed chart is computed in the Placidian plane, but the planets are then placed in the chart in the plane of the earth's orbit, which is mathematically incommensurable. What would happen if the planets were re-computed in the same plane as that in which the chart is drawn? Insofar as we know, this has never been tried, but there is some hint that Johndro was experimenting with such a system prior to his death. We are not sure. This would entail a very complicated set of recalculations. The question is, would progressions work if they were correctly calculated? They are not correctly calculated at the present time, because you can't take planetary positions from an ephemeris calculated in one plane of space and apply them to another plane of space. That is what the progressionists are doing now. There is no question in our minds that the progressionists are partly in error, but we hesitate to say they are ALL wrong...It is our advice to the student to stick to transits insofar as every day practice is concerned, but to experiment with progressions or anything else as much as you like, AFTER you have mastered transits. We hope the student will avoid any dogma...Each side has been unable to listen to arguments on the other side. If that is not where progressions end, it is where progress ends...

Coming back to progressions, our conclusion is that they are inaccurate. We do not claim that the idea of progressions is wrong or that there is no foundation for them... Thus, although we have found progressions inaccurate a good part of the time, our own investigations lead us to the suspicion that we might make a very serious error if we were to throw them away altogether.

In working with transits, so long as the natal chart and the planets are in the same plane of space, you have a relatively simple matter to deal with. Astronomical tables are accurate. You know where the planets are."

10. Lehman, J. Lee, *Classical Solar Returns*, Schiffer Books, Pennelvania, 2012, p.29

"When I see a method that gleefully generates four different charts to serve the same function, I have to question how predictive any of them be on a regular basis because otherwise why would you need all four? If you need this many multiple choices, then none of them is giving you enough information for prediction, and you are just throwing in random events in the hopes that one of them will be explanatory after the fact. You might as well throw in the towel, and admit that you have no method...it simply guarantees a system in which ambiguity and confusion is preferred over any kind of prediction whatsoever."

11. http://en.wikipedia.org/wiki/Orbital_node
12. Boehrer, Kt, *Declination, the Other Dimension*, Fortunata Press, 1994.
13. Ibid., p.71-73.
14. http://www.forrestastrology.com/resources/articles/general-astrology/215-the-out-of-bounds-moon
15. Gibson M.D., Mitchell E., *Signs of Mental Illness*, Llewellyn Publications, 1998.
16. Ibid, p. 58.
17. Oscar Pistorius' friend recounts gunshot incident at restauranthttp://www.usatoday.com/story/sports/olympics/2014/03/05/oscar-pistorius-trial/6059841/
18. http://en.wikipedia.org/wiki/Arab_Spring#Egypt
    "The 15 October 2011 global protests and the Occupy Wall Street movement, which started in the United States and has since spread to Asia and Europe, drew direct inspiration from the Arab Spring, with organizers asking U.S. citizens "Are you ready for a Tahrir moment?" The protesters have committed to using the "revolutionary Arab Spring tactic" to achieve their goals of curbing corporate power and control in Western governments."
19. http://www.historyorb.com/events/date/2011
20. http://www.bbc.com/news/blogs-trending-28782308
21. The Solar Parts chart is generated by software AstroDeluxe by John Halloran at http://www.halloran.com/
22. http://www.bbc.com/news/world-middle-east-26248275

Precession
and the Age of Aquarius

Precession is the slow movement of the stars against our seasons measured from the spring solstice in modern times. Traditionally this cycle is determined by the location of the sun in one of the twelve zodiac constellations at the vernal equinox, which corresponds to the moment the sun rises above the celestial equator at 0 Aries, marking the start of spring in the northern hemisphere each year. It's a cycle of 25,950 years that can be subdivided into twelve ages and was first identified by ancient Egyptians as long ago as 10,500 BC. The Ages move backward through the zodiac constellations averaging about 2,160 years for each Age.

I believe we are currently in the Age of Aquarius and though much has been written about when the beginning of the Age of Aquarius starts, most of it has been confusing because of the constellations of Pisces and Aquarius overlap. This is because modern authors are only using modern astronomical techniques of measuring the sky with the 1929 IAU divisions of the constellations and only looking at the spring equinox.

Astrologers do not agree on when the Aquarian age will start or even if it has already started. Nick Campion in his book, The Book of World Horoscopes, listed 29 astrological references for the start of the Age of Aquarius arriving in the 20th century, the second place was the 24th century with twelve claimants.

This is a contentious issue amongst astrologers because the major problem with the constellation of Pisces is it is more than 45 degrees wide, and it overlaps the constellation of Aquarius. The Northern Fish is to the left of Aquarius but the Southern Fish is under the constellation of Aquarius. Where does one begin and the other end when these two constellations overlap each other? Note that Formalhaut (one of the Persian Royal Stars) is currently allocated in Piscis Austrinus, the Southern Fish of Pisces but it used to belong to Aquarius.[2]

It is a mistake to only place our focus on Aquarius at the spring equinox. Only analyzing this one point just leads to many opinions when the constellation of Pisces overlays the constellation of Aquarius. Looking back to ancient astronomical images and monuments point to another solution.

Stars aligned with the Spring Solstice over Time[1]

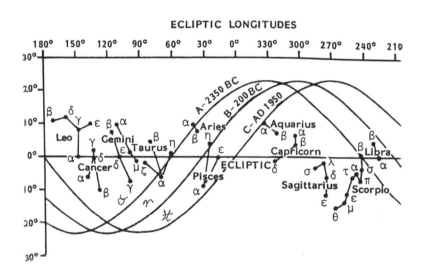

Ecliptic Longitude Over Time

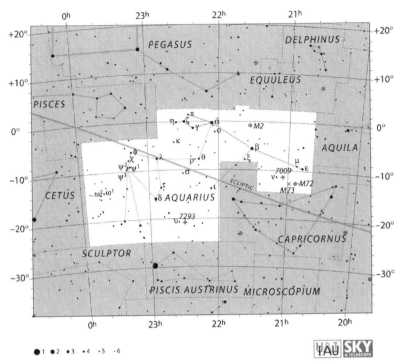

Constellation of Aquarius[3]

Our European culture generally gives Hipparchus (190-120 BCE) credit for measuring precession. He measured it as a degree for each century but we currently place precession at one degree every 72 years (a very important number). Yet Hipparchus pointed to the Egyptians and said 'the Egyptian priests are supreme in the science of the sky' and it was they that 'revealed to the Greeks the secrets of the full year [precession]'. Another Greek, Herodotus (c.450 BC) also pointed to the knowledge of the Egyptians and wrote that it was 'at Heliopolis that the most learned of the Egyptians are to be found...all agree in saying that the Egyptians by their study of astronomy discovered the solar year and were the first to divide it into twelve parts'.[4] To solve this disputed problem, we need to look to how the Egyptians measured the sky.

The Ancients of Egypt and Babylon didn't use these modern AIU divisions between constellations. It was visual astronomy. There are many ways to measure and observe the sky and the Egyptians were expert observers over thousands of years. They measured the movement of the sky in multiple ways, not just looking only at the horizon on the first day of spring. They followed the circumpolar stars, they measured their 10 day weeks by the rising stars at night (star decans). They measured the day hours with water clocks. They knew the circumference of the earth by measuring the shadow differences between obelisks many miles apart. Thanks in large part to their accuracy in measuring precession, they were able to realigned the temples to Isis as the star Sirius moved because of precession. They built monuments in the Age of Taurus and temples adorned with rams in the Age of Aries.

As a testament to their astronomical prowess, the Egyptians created Heaven on Earth with their entire country and they believed 'as above, so below'. Robert Bauval points out in *The Orion Mystery* that Osiris (Egypt's great myth of resurrection of the Pharaoh) was represented by the constellation of Orion. The Great Pyramids of Giza were the equivalent of Orion's Belt. The ancient Egyptians tracked the declination of the Orion constellation for thousands of years as another way to measure precession. According to Bauval, they united upper and lower Egypt around 2400 BC when Orion elevated above the equator at Memphis. They measured the sky in many directions for thousands of years.

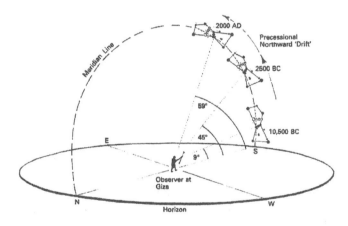

The effect of Orion's slow precessional slide up the meridian between 10,500 BC and 2500 BC is that the constellation would literally have appeared to be 'drifting' very slowly northwards along the course of the Milky Way.

Orion Constellation declination
from The Message of the Sphinx[5]

The Sphinx itself may provide another support of the long history of Egyptians measurement of the sky. Dr. Robert Schoch, a professor of geology at Boston University stated in 1990 that he believed the body of the Sphinx was much older than Egyptologists believed. He dated the Sphinx's back to 7,000 – 9,000 BC because of water erosion of the Sphinx's body and its surrounding enclosure. Dr Schoch as a geologist didn't get into precession theory but his findings help confirm Bauval's theory that the Sphinx was carved out of the existing rock formation prior to the time that Giza area became a desert.[6] This corresponds to Bauval's theories. Bauval shows that the Sphinx is likely to go back to 10,500 BC as it looked at the 'First Time' or Egyptian 'Tep Zepi' when the constellation of Leo rose on the spring solstice. The head of the Sphinx has been modified several times but Bauval believes the original head was that of a Lion looking at Leo rising on the horizon during the Age of Leo. He believes that the Egyptians were trying to mark their beliefs of the 'First Time' for the ages along with the alignment of the Great Pyramids to Orion's Belt.

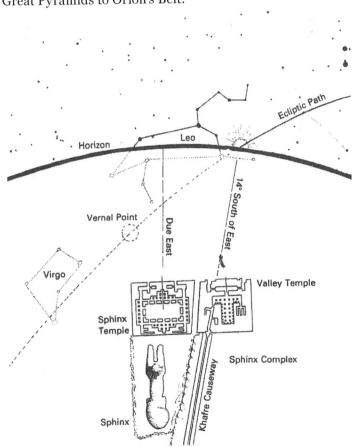

**The 'First Time' (Tep Zepi) 10,500 BC
from The Message of the Sphinx[7]**

As noted earlier, the Egyptians measured precession in many directions and they looked to the circumpolar stars too. They tracked what star was on or near the geographic North Pole in addition to the constellation on the horizon. During the Age of Taurus, it was again the constellation of Leo rising this time at the Summer Solstice, the beginning of the Egyptian New Year. This was the last period when the Sun was in tropical Cancer while the constellation Leo was on the horizon at Summer Solstice at the same time. Stecchini stated in *Secrets of the Great Pyramid*:

> [Referring to the facing lions at the grave circle at Mycenae] "The two lions which face each other on the sides of the column represent a circle closing on itself. The easiest way to convey the meaning of this symbol is to refer to pieces of ancient jewelry which consist of a bracelet open at one side with the head of a lion on each open end. The lions represent the summer solstice. The stance of the lions, with the front paws on the line of the tropic and their hind paws extending below it (this stance will later become the heraldic symbol of the lion rampant), indicates the spread of the zodiacal band north and south of the ecliptic. The ancients established their astronomical system when the spring equinox was in Taurus, which ceased to be true at the beginning of the second millennium B.C."

During the Age of Taurus, the star Theban, in the constellation of Drago, was at the geographic North Pole. Currently the star Polaris points to the geographic North Pole.

We can see this same image from the Zodiac of Temple of Dendera where the Egyptians distinguished between the geographic north pole and the ecliptic north pole. They followed the stars that marked the geographic north pole as another form of measuring precession.

The images on the the next page suggest that the Egyptians and other cultures didn't just measure only one point. Historically each solstice and equinox was measured along with the midpoint of each season. We see this across cultures where the cardinal directions are noted with the cross-quarter days becoming holidays, like All Saints Day and May Day.[10]

The Giza Causeways of all three pyramids mark these same eight measurements with 14 degree angles and 28 degree angles to mark the path of the Sun through the eight points in a solar year.

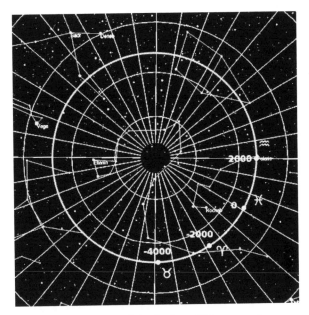

North Geographic Pole of Precession

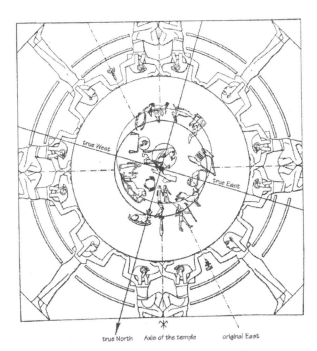

**Drawing of the Dendera Zodiac
from Secrets of the Great Pyramid[9]**

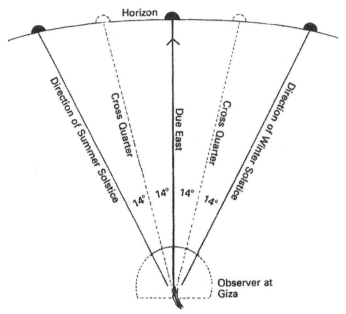

Sunrise at Giza from The Orion Mystery

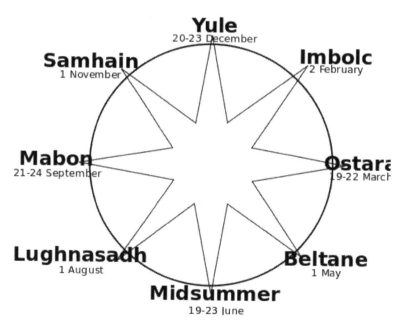

Measuring the Solar Year[11]

The Assyrian Lamassu at the Oriental Institute Museum at the University of Chicago[13]

Jesus Christ within Viscia Pisces and the Fixed Cross

It was common among ancient cultures to mark or measure each and every season. During the Age of Taurus many cultures marked the beginning of spring and the vernal equinox with the Pleiades in the constellation of Taurus. They used the constellations of Taurus, Leo, Scorpio and Aquarius to mark spring, summer, fall and winter. These four constellations are particularly important because they carried the four Royal Stars[12] of Aldebaran, Regulus, Antares, and Fomulhaut. These four stars were used to measure time. They are unique in that they are almost exactly 90 degrees apart and lay close to the ecliptic. Which means that as one is rising in the east, one is culminating overhead while another is setting in the west. They are perfect for measuring the nightly hours, the seasons and precession.

It was during this Age of Taurus when the association of kingship, rulership and dominion was made with these four constellations that were also used to mark the four seasons of a solar year. During this period, kings or rulers associated themselves with the stars and celestial authority. They continued to carry this association with dominion, kingship and rulership across the ages with these four constellations.

To represent this authority or dominion the Assyians created a mythic creator that was part bull (Taurus), lion (Leo), eagle (another form of Scorpio) and man (Aquarius).

This same motif of authority or dominion is carried into the Age of Pisces in medieval churches with Jesus Christ surrounded by the four evangelists shown as the animals of the bull, lion, eagle and man.

The two images on the previous page show this association of rulership in the Age of Taurus and the Age of Pisces. It was the importance of these four stars to measure time and precession that dominion and kingship continued to be used with the four constellations of Taurus, Leo, Scorpio and Aquarius. They are the clues to answering the question. Are we in the Age of Aquarius? It is necessary to look at each constellation rising for every equinox and solstice. This will give us the answer to this lingering question.

Below are the seasons for 2014 set for Austin, Texas exactly 70 minutes before sunrise. The Sun needs to be 17 degrees below the horizon in order to see the constellation on the horizon. The view is basely the same as Cairo, Egypt but the time of sunrise is slightly different. For our purpose, this difference is not significant. These four constellations can measure precession any place in the northern hemisphere between the Arctic Circle and the Equator. The Cairo images have the sun exactly on the horizon to show the position of the sun with the constellation.[14]

**Scorpio Constellation on horizon at the Winter Solstice
December 21, 2013 at 6:13 am at Austin**

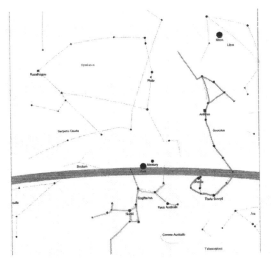

Beginning of
Fixed Cross
Scorpio
Winter 2000
Cairo

**Scorpio Constellation on horizon
at the Winter Solstice at Cairo 2000**

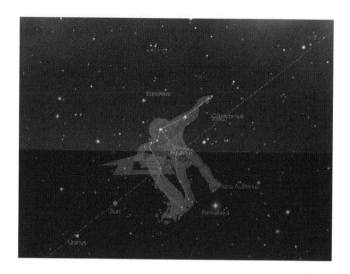

**Aquarius Constellation on horizon at the Spring Equinox
March 20, 2014 at 6:25 am at Austin**

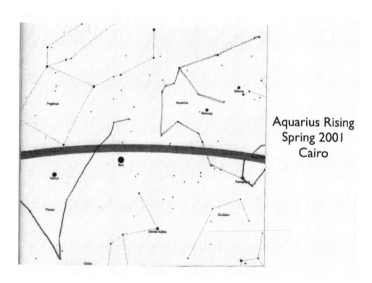

Aquarius Rising
Spring 2001
Cairo

**Aquarius Constellation on horizon
at the Spring Equinox at Cairo**

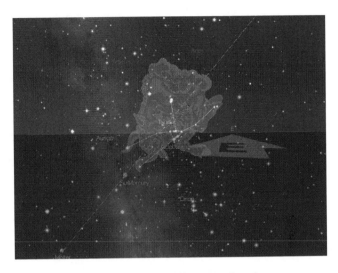

Taurus Constellation on horizon
at the Summer Solstice June 22, 2014 at 5:20 am at Austin

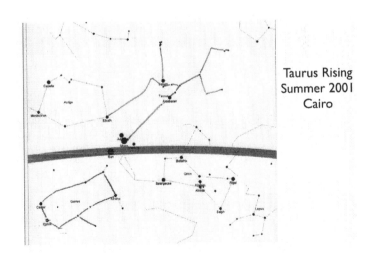

Taurus Rising
Summer 2001
Cairo

Taurus Constellation on horizon
at the Summer Solstice at Cairo 2001

**Leo Constellation on horizon
at the Fall Equinox March 20, 2014 at 6:09 am at Austin**

Leo Rising
Fall 2001
Cairo

**Leo Constellation on horizon
at the Fall Equinox at Cairo 2001**

It is clear without a doubt in my mind that we are already in the Age of Aquarius because all four constellations of Aquarius, Taurus, Leo and Scorpio are on the horizon at the beginning of each season. They now mark the solstices and equinoxes. It is also clear that all four of the constellations associated with Pisces (the Mutable signs of Sagittarius, Virgo and Gemini) have sunk below the horizon. They are no longer visible on the solstices or equinoxes. All four have passed out of view. They have been sinking below the horizon for over a century.

Some esotericists believed that the comet of 1881 was a portent for the coming Age.[15] What are the characteristics or nature of Aquarius? It is a fact that society and progress has speeded up since the Second Industrial Revolution (1840-1870). The many inventions of the mid to late 19th century like the steam engine, electricity and the migration of farming into the cities of industry are just a few of the milestones that have changed society. They are the hallmark of the nature of Aquarius, the sign of inventions. The 20th century continued progress with the inventions of the automobile and communication; the telegraph, telephone, radio and television. Society changed exponentially, another characteristic of Aquarius. By the mid 20th century we moved into the computerized age and the space program. In the 1980's we had home computers from miniaturization. In the last decade of the 20th century, the creation of the Internet started to shrink the globe so that everyone could be connected. These are all associated with Aquarius.

We are barely into this new Age but the signs are clear that we have been leaving behind the Piscean Age with each century. The great hold that our current religions held over governments and people has diminished. They are fading into the background of society. The heads of religion can no longer dictate to kings or rulers. They can only advise.

Below are images from prior ages to show their symbolism. But what next will be the symbol for this new Age of Aquarius?

Age of Taurus
4480 BC

The Age of Taurus

Entrance to Temple of Karnak
Ram Headed Sphinxes
Age of Aries

The Age of Aries

Age of Pisces
The Fishes

The Age of Pisces

Joseph Campbell thought the image for this new Age should be the Blue Marble floating in space. He believed this century needed a modern representation to match this sense of unity and globalization. One world, no boundaries, we are all of the Earth.[16]

A New Global Image, a World without Borders

Or perhaps this modern Aquarius by Florinda Leighton 1976:

A Modern Aquarius[17]

I believe the world has been slipping into this new Age of Aquarius since the 19th century since so many inventions have been developed that have changed society dramatically around the globe. Even in the most remote areas of the globe, there are cell phones. It is clear from measuring the constellations on all equinoxes and solstices that the Age of Pisces is no longer visible on the horizon with the beginning of the seasons. The question has been answered. The changes in our culture since the Industrial Revolution clearly point to this truth. The power of technology is changing the perception of our worldview, political structures and society. We are in this transition and we are only just in the early stage of this 2,160 year Age of Aquarius.

Footnotes

1. http://en.wikipedia.org/wiki/Precession author Kevin Heagen, Wikipedia Commons
2. http://en.wikipedia.org/wiki/Fomalhaut Fomalhaut can be located in these northern latitudes by the fact that the western (right-hand) side of the Square of Pegasus points to it. Continue the line from Beta to Al-

pha Pegasi towards the southern horizon: Fomalhaut is about 45° south of Alpha Pegasi, with no bright stars in between...In Greek mythology, this constellation is known as the Great Fish and it is portrayed as swallowing the water being poured out by Aquarius, the water-bearer constellation. The two fish of the constellation Pisces are said to be the offspring of the Great Fish.

3. http://en.wikipedia.org/wiki/File:Aquarius_IAU.svg author: IAU and Sky & Telescope magazine (Roger Sinnott & Rick Fienberg) Wiki Commons

4. Radice, B. (advisory ed.) Herodotus. *The Histories.* Penguin Books, London, 1972 ed., II 2-8.

5. Hancock, Graham and Bauvel, Robert, *The Message of the Sphinx*, Crown Publishers, Inc., New York 1996, page 231.

6. http://www.robertschoch.com/sphinxcontent.html

7. Hancock, *The Message of the Sphinx*, op.cit., p. 261

8. http://en.wikipedia.org/wiki/North_Star author: Tom Ruen Dbachmann, Wikipedia Commons

9. Tomkins, Peter, *Secrets of the Great Pyramid*, p.173

10. Hancock, *The Message of the Sphinx*, op.cit., p. 255.

11. http://en.wikipedia.org/wiki/Wheel_of_the_Year

12. http://en.wikipedia.org/wiki/Royal stars   The four stars with their modern and ancient Persian names were:**Aldebaran** (Tascheter) - vernal equinox (Watcher of the East) **Regulus** (Venant) - summer solstice (Watcher of the North) **Antares** (Satevis) - autumnal equinox **Fomalhaut** (Haftorang/Hastorang) - winter solstice (Watcher of the South) The four dominant stars have an apparent magnitude of 1.5 or less. The reason why they are called "Royal" is that they appear to stand aside from the other stars in the sky. The four stars, Aldebaran, Regulus, Antares, Formalhaut are the brightest stars in their constellations, as well as being part of the twenty five brightest stars in the sky, and were considered the four guardians of the heaven. They marked the seasonal changes of the year and marked the equinoxes and ...By 700 BCE the Nineveh and Assyrians had essentially mapped the ecliptic cycle because of the four stars and were in result able to map the constellations, distinguishing them from the planets and the fixed stars. From this, in 747 BCE the Babylonian King Nau-nasir adopted a calendar derived from information based on the four stars, one following an eight-year cycle and one a nineteen-year cycle (later adopting the nineteen-year calendar as standard) Fomalhaut watched the Southern sky and was the brightest star in Piscis Austrinus (sharing the same longitude with the star Sadalmelik which is the predominant star in Aquarius).

13. http://en.wikipedia.org/wiki/File:Lammasu.jpg This is the Assyrian Lamassu at the Oriental Institute Museum at the University of Chicago. Gypsum (?) Khorsabad, entrance to the throne room Neo-Assyrian Period, ca. 721-705 B.C. OIM A7369. The lamassu is a celestial being from Mesopotamian mythology. Human above the waist and a bull below the waist, it also has the horns and the ears of a bull. It appears frequently in Mesopotamian art, sometimes with wings. The lamassu and shedu were household protective spirits of the common Babylonian

people, becoming associated later as royal protectors, were placed as sentinels at the entrances. (This reference omitted a lion's body. The British Museum shows one with Lion's feet)

14. I used the StarWalk App for the ipad 2014. Note the Sun below the horizon at 17 degrees. For the 2001 images, Skyglobe for Windows was used.

15. Ovason, David, *The Secret Architecture of Our Nation's Capitol.* Harper Collins Publishers, New York 2000, p.34. (as a side note, this was the year of Franklin D. Roosevelt's birth) Its brightest day was near the summer solstice of June 22, 1881.

16. http://i.space.com/images/i/000/028/215/i02/earth-day-image-2013-13.jpg?1366642652

17. Leighton, Florinda, 1976 Aquarius fused glass on copper, owned by Naomi Bennett.

Conclusions

The major purpose of this book is to aid our astrological community in re-discovering its roots and foundations. This search for what is functional and what really works is a goal that most of the western 20th century astrologers have been pursuing for over 100 years. They saw the value and truth in astrology but they also knew there was a great deal of error, un-reliability and inconsistency. However astrology functioned enough that they could not drop it as hearsay or bunk. The new translations of the ancient texts in the past 30 years have been an extension of the search for functionality, but there are also discoveries that are valuable from the 'modern' astrologers like Charles Jayne, Sydney K. Bennett, Grant Lewi and Carl Payne Tobey. The Germans added planetary pictures and midpoints which is a modern form of Arabic Parts. Now is the time for synthesis.

I was trained in most of the geometric principles laid out in this book back in 1969. I studied the Hellenistic Greeks with Project Hindsight and Robert Hand. I was also doing other independent research to find the necessary source material to confirm astrology's structure and the source of its foundation that was uncovered by Tobey. It took time to find new references outside of the written astrological tradition that is directly related to the origins of astrology. They are limited and I hope with additional discoveries made in archeoastronomy, more will be made. There is still an exaggerated reverence for the Greeks in our western culture that is still present in western astrology. I hope that more value will be placed with the older cultures before the Greeks. Sadly there is little evidence left since it was standard practice that conquerors destroyed the prior knowledge by killing the priests and rulers that kept the records.

The re-discovery of the Hellenistic methods have created a large community of astrologers re-examining astrology's origins. In addition to the resurgence of Hellenistic methods, very recently there has also been a new acceptance of using Whole Sign Houses in the astrological community instead of the Quadrant Houses. This is major step forward in solving the problem of chart construction. Letting the midheaven become a chart point solves the difficulty of reconciling the difference between geographic and ecliptic measurements.

I am hopeful that a re-examination of sign and house rulership that is presented in this book can become a re-discovery of the geometric principles that were designed into the structure of astrology from its beginning. It has not been stated directly in the prior chapters but the entire horoscope is mostly a collection of mathematical points such as the ascendant, house divisions, midheaven and lunar nodes. Technically, even the entire zodiac is just a mathematical plane that has no material, physical existence just as the Earth's equator is just a mathematical line or plane. Astrology is the expression of geometric form applied to life on Earth and life follows geometric form as demonstrated in the Fibonacci numbers and fractal geometry.

With regards to sign and house rulership, Helenistic planetary order shows that **average mean distance from Earth** is the basis of sign rulerships. With this principle in mind, there is no question that Pluto should be assigned to Aries and that there are two remaining rulers beyond Pluto to be assigned to Taurus and Gemini. Eris is a definite candidate to be studied. Any use of asteroids between Mars and Jupiter cannot have rulership of the signs since it violates the principle of average mean distance.

The house functions that were identified by the Hellenistic Greeks are still being used today with little modification. The ancients were obsessed with the rotation of the earth against the vault of the sky and it was this constant daily motion that formed the basis of the duality between signs and houses. This duality is reflected with the division of the Sun and Moon with the signs listed with the co-rulership of planets of Mercury to Saturn. This is a hidden geometric pattern of sign and house rulership. The pattern behind them is clearly aligned to the Leo House Count. This house rulership that starts with Leo and ends with Virgo fits perfectly with both Traditional and Modern house characteristics. The Aries House Count was a recent invention in the past century that clearly doesn't fit.

I have not found an external geometric reference for the assignment of Aspects to House Rulership but the Ptolemaic aspects do appear to fit the pattern that Tobey discovered. It now appears that Rob Hand may be coming close to this conclusion too but from a very different perspective.[1]

There is a mystery of harmonic relationships of angle and resonance that has relevance to life on Earth that modern science has been discovering and these reflect the principles that the ancients put into their religions and myths. I do not believe there will ever be a material explanation of astrology by the use of gravity. But harmonics, angle and resonance described by fractal geometry, music and sound (which is just a form of vibration) is a possibility. Modern science is still in its infancy but I firmly believe that astrology's structure and basis will be discovered in the future if only academic bias can be removed. All of the current scientific discoveries that are related to the cycles of the Sun and Moon to life on Earth are astrological. They just cannot use the A-word.

I look forward to the post-modern integration of the traditional astrology with the modern.1 This is a trend that will take this neo-astrology into the 21st century. I hope this book will be valuable addition to the integration of the old with the new.

Footnotes

1. Hand, Robert "An Interview with Robert Hand, the Integration of Modern and Traditional Astrology", *The Mountain Astrology Magazine*, Oct/Nov. 2014.

   Tem Tarriktar: You mentioned that you are going to be addressing house relationships in this new book [in 2015]..."

   Rob Hand: Yes, I'm addressing the issue of aspects being a form of house relationships. For example, sextiles are 3rd-house and 11th-house aspects, which means they impinge on things that the 3rd and 11th houses impinge on, in a more general way. The houses are much more specific. **But I think the aspects and the houses all arise out of the sign relationships...**
   Let me give an example. In this system, **the benevolent houses make aspects to the Ascendant!** Or more precisely, the malevolent aspects make no aspects to the Ascendant, which is more to the point. And the whole business of turning the wheel and using derived house meanings is so much more reasonable, because you **actually see in that process that houses, aspects, and so forth are all products of sign relationships...**

   Chris Brennan: And then once you found Whole Sign houses circa 1992–93, or at least you confirmed that it was in all the Hellenistic texts, suddenly house division made sense to you, and it's something that became a core part of your astrology.

   RH: Yes, the 2nd house really does rule money and other things you're attached to. Specifically, I had no way of finding out whether a person was likely to be poverty-stricken or make a decent living, and between the proper use of the 2nd house, the Part of Fortune, and the Place of Acquisition ... oh, yes, now I can...

I use Whole Sign houses, period. The closest I come to blending quadrant thinking is that I consider the sign of the Midheaven to be as powerful in determining professions as the 10th house...

Interpreting my chart correctly is a mess, using later systems of house division, but it completely makes sense when you use Whole Sign houses. You always start with your own chart, but I've had enough experience, using this house system with literally thousands of clients, to be confident of it...

I think that's the future. **I cannot guarantee that the synthesis will be entirely along the lines I am suggesting, but some kind of synthesis is the future.** The only modern astrology — or it would be more accurate to say "20th-century astrology," because I think what we're actually talking about here is the new modern astrology — the only 20th-century forms of astrology that we will not be able to reconcile with traditional astrology are ones that have made very specific technical commitments to things that are peculiar to the 20th century, like Neptune ruling Pisces — you know, the rulerships — and I would also say quadrant houses fall into this category. The quadrant houses, in some form or other, may have a future, as I have mentioned, particularly regarding the quantitative intensity of a planet. I do not think they have a future as an indication of signification, however. If they do, someone had better come up with a theoretical justification. **But even then, we still have the main theoretical problem that has dogged all of us from Rhetorius forward, which is: Which quadrant house system?** The modern rulerships of the signs of the zodiac, employing Uranus, Neptune, and Pluto, are derived from principles that are completely alien to the original foundation of planetary rulerships by essential dignity...

What if we're testing the wrong kind of astrology? **Maybe it's not that astrology is incorrect, but our astrology is incorrect.**

References

Bennett, Naomi, "*Why Hellenistic Planetary Order?,*" International Society of Astrological Research Journal, Vol. 43, No. 1, April 2014.

Bennett, Sydney K.(aka Wynn), *The Key Cycle* by Wynn, American Federation of Astrologers 1970.

Boehrer, Kt, *Declination, the Other Dimension*, Fortunata Press, 1994.

Collins, Andrew, Gödekli Tepe, *Genesis of the Gods*, Bear and Company, Vermont, 2014

Crowley, Aleister, *The General Principles of Astrology*, edited by Hymenaeus Beta, Weiser Books, Boston, 2002 (originally 1927).

Desroches-Noblecort, Christiane, "Le Zodiaque de Pharaon", *Archeologia* Numero 292, Juillet-Aout 1993, pages 21-4

Gibson M.D., Mitchell E., *Signs of Mental Illness*, Llewellyn Publications, 1998.

Hancock, Graham and Bauvel, Robert, *The Message of the Sphinx*, Crown Publishers, Inc., New York 1996.

Hand, Robert, "An Interview with Robert Hand, the Integration of Modern and Traditional Astrology", *The Mountain Astrology Magazine*, Oct/Nov. 2014.

Hand, Robert, "A Study in Early House Division," The Astrological Association Journal, London July 1997.

Hand, Robert, "*Towards a Post-Modern Astrology,*" Astrological Conference 2005 of the British Astrological Association in York, UK. 2005

Holden, James H., *Biographical Dictionary of Western Astrologers*, A.F.A., 2013

Houlding, Deborah, *The Houses, Temples of the Sky*, Wessex Astrologer, Bournemouth, England, 2006, Forward by Robert Hand.
Holden, James H., Section on Fifth Period Modern Astrology, *A History of Horoscopic Astrology*, American Federation of Astrology, 2006.

Lehman, J. Lee, *Classical Solar Returns*, Schiffer Books, Pennelvania, 2012.

Lehman, Lee. *Essential Dignities*, Whitford Press, 1989.

Lewi, Grant, *Astrology for the Millions*, Llewellyn Publications, St.Paul, MN, 1969.

Lewi, Grant, *Heaven Knows What*, Llewellyn Publications 1969.

Lawlor, Robert L., *Sacred Geometry*, Thames & Hudson, London 1982

Ovason, David, *The Secret Architecture of Our Nation's Capitol.* Harper Collins Publishers, New York 2000.

Radice, B. (advisory ed.) Herodotus. *The Histories.* Penguin Books, London, 1972 ed.

Raphael's Astronomical Ephemeris of the Planets' Places for 1901, W Foulsham & Co., Ltd, London, UK.,

Schmidt, Robert. "House Division, Planetary Strength, and Cusps in Hellenistic Astrology." This is in the introduction to Book III of the Tetrabiblos translated by Robert Schmidt for Project Hindsight, with the permission of Keith J. Williams of the Traditions Mail List, 1997.

Stecchini, Livio Catullo, Appendix of Notes on the Relation of Ancient Measures to the Great Pyramid, *Secrets of The Great Pyramid*, 1971, Harper and Row, New York, p. 287-382.

Tobey, Carl Payne, *Astrology of Inner Space*, Omen Press, Tucson 1972.

Tobey, Carl Payne, Collected Works of Carl Payne Tobey, Bonami Inc, Texas 1998.

Tobey, Carl Payne, Correspondence Course, 1957.

Wikipedia for many subjects such as fractal geometry, precession and public domain images.

Astrological Symbols

Planets		Keywords	Zodiacal Signs	
☽	Moon	emotional, self survival	♋	Cancer
☉	Sun	energetic self expression	♌	Leo
☿	Mercury	mental practical work/service	♍	Virgo
♀	Venus	attraction between people	♎	Libra
♂	Mars	sexuality, loyalty, driveness	♏	Scorpio
♃	Jupiter	energetic abundant opportunity	♐	Sagittarius
♄	Saturn	limits, duty, responsibility	♑	Capricorn
♅	Uranus	original, explosive, abrupt	♒	Aquarius
♆	Neptune	imagination, fantasy, sympathy	♓	Pisces
♇	Pluto	energy, drive, obsession	♈	Aries
♀	Venus	stability, stubborn, luxury	♉	Taurus
☿	Mercury	quick, humorous, ideas	♊	Gemini
☊	Lunar Node	impulsive, unexpected		

Aspects (angles) between planets

☌	0°	Conjunction	neutral, depends on the planets and sign
✳	60°	Sextile	compatible, gets along easily, communicating, social
⌄	30	Semi-sextile	fearful, lack energy, passive
□	90°	Square	tension, conflict, frustration, demands, stress
△	120°	Trine	energetic, creative, vibrant, exciting
⚻	150°	Quincunx	weak, lack of energy, sickly, off balance
☍	180°	Opposition	tension, stress, 3rd parties, torn in two directions

Other Symbols Used in Astrology

n	natal planet	Rx	retrograde motion of a planet
t	transit of a planet to a natal chart	||	Parallel: same declination of

Dual Rulership of Signs and Houses

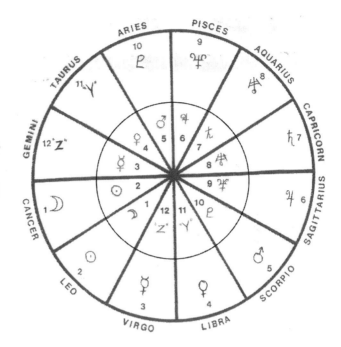

Rulerships of Duality
Sign and House

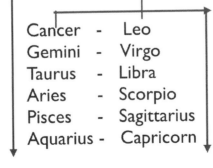

Moon	Cancer	-	Leo	Sun
Mercury	Gemini	-	Virgo	Mercury
Venus	Taurus	-	Libra	Venus
Pluto	Aries	-	Scorpio	Mars
Neptune	Pisces	-	Sagittarius	Jupiter
Uranus	Aquarius	-	Capricorn	Saturn

78031463R00093

Made in the USA
Columbia, SC
08 October 2017